GREAT WRITERS **J.R.R. TOLKIEN**

GREAT WRITERS

J.R.R. TOLKIEN

Neil Heims

Foreword by Colin Duriez

CHELSEA HOUSE
PUBLISHERS
A Haights Cross Communications Company
Philadelphia

CHELSEA HOUSE PUBLISHERS

VP, NEW PRODUCT DEVELOPMENT Sally Cheney
DIRECTOR OF PRODUCTION Kim Shinners
CREATIVE MANAGER Takeshi Takahashi
MANUFACTURING MANAGER Diann Grasse

Staff for J.R.R. TOLKIEN

EXECUTIVE EDITOR: Matt Uhler
ASSOCIATE EDITOR: Susan Naab
EDITORIAL ASSISTANT: Sharon Slaughter
PRODUCTION EDITOR: Megan Emery
SERIES AND COVER DESIGNER: Takeshi Takahashi
LAYOUT: EJB Publishing Services
COVER: © Bettmann/CORBIS

A Haights Cross Communications Company

http://www.chelseahouse.com

First Printing

9 8 7 6 5 4 3 2 1

Library of Congress Cataloging-in-Publication Data

Heims, Neil.
  J.R.R. Tolkien / by Neil Heims.
    v. cm. — (Great writers)
  Includes bibliographical references and index.
  Contents: A career begins — Boyhood — Internal resources — At Leeds
and Oxford — Family — Fellowship — Authorship — War, politics, and
religion — Culminations.
  ISBN 0-7910-7847-7
  1. Tolkien, J. R. R. (John Ronald Reuel), 1892-1973. 2. Fantasy literature,
English—History and criticism. 3. Authors, English—20th century—Biog-
raphy. 4. Philologists—Great Britain—Biography. 5. Middle Earth
(Imaginary place) [1. Tolkien, J. R. R. (John Ronald Reuel), 1892-1973. 2.
Authors, English.] I. Title. II. Great writers (Philadelphia, Pa.)
  PR6039.O32Z657 2004
  828'.91209—dc22

                                              2003028172

▮▮▮▮ TABLE OF CONTENTS

IN THIS ENGAGING BIOGRAPHY, Neil Heims recounts the story of a reporter asking J.R.R. Tolkien what "made him tick". Tolkien retorted that he did not tick—he was not a machine.

Tolkien was a complex character, a gift and a challenge to the biographer. He is a gift because of his depth and colour as an individual. He vividly lives. Whether the focus is upon Tolkien the young child, the boy, the young man thrust into the death-pits of World War One and the Battle of the Somme, the aspiring scholar, the learned Professor at Oxford, Tolkien is recognizable. He is himself and no other. But he is also a challenge to the biographer, as so much of his life (in terms of what is interesting and memorable for others to read about) resides in his mind and imagination. He is not a man of action. Outwardly his life often appears routine and even monotonous. This compact book embraces both the gift and the challenge of Tolkien, presenting an accessible portrait of the man and a reliable and useful insight for the general reader into the inner workings of his complex mind.

Like his close friend C.S. Lewis, Tolkien intensely disliked the critical trend (the "personal heresy", Lewis called it) which focused upon the psychology of the author to the detriment of the subject's work. (No doubt much of what is written about him today Tolkien would have regarded as, to use his word, "impertinence"). *J.R.R. Tolkien: A Literary Biography* tells Tolkien's life with the purpose of illuminating the works, particularly *The Hobbit*, *The Lord of the Rings*, and *The Silmarillion*. It is in fact merely because of the global popularity of the works, particularly *The Lord of the Rings*, that people have become interested in the man, who became a celebrity only towards the end of his life, much to his bemusement and sometimes annoyance (as when he got phone calls from enthusiastic American readers, unaware of the time difference, in the early hours of the morning). On one occasion Tolkien attended a dull public lecture at Oxford by the writer Robert Graves, which was also attended by the film star Ava Gardner. As the three—Graves, Tolkien and Gardner—left the building, the flash bulbs of the Press attended to the actress, ignoring the man who, as far as the media then was concerned, did not exist.

It is one of the deepest ironies of literary history that Tolkien, known only to specialists in early English language and literature, took up a fantasy genre considered then only to be suitable for children—the fairy story, or elvish tale. Almost single-handedly he re-created an adult readership for it. In the process he enlisted the help of his friend C.S. Lewis, who wrote science-fiction, belonging to the same family of "romance"—that is, stories that provide tantalizing glimpses of other worlds, and that make a direct appeal to the imagination in their wonder and strangeness. Without Tolkien's project there would be no Fantasy sections in today's bookstores, perhaps no visible sign of Ursula Le Guin, or Terry Pratchett, or Orson Scott Card. Certainly, of course, New Zealand would not have become Middle-earth (Tolkien's original The Shire having been lost for ever in the creeping urban spread of Birmingham in the English Midlands). Vast audiences around the planet would have been deprived of Peter Jackson's brilliant film rendition of *The Lord of the Rings*.

When he reviewed the newly published *The Return of the King* in the *New York Times* on January 22, 1956, W.H. Auden bemoaned Tolkien's ability to divide his readers.

In "The Return of the King," Frodo Baggins fulfills his Quest, the realm of Sauron is ended forever, the Third Age is over and J. R. R. Tolkien's trilogy "The Lord of the Rings" complete. I rarely remember a book about which I have had such violent arguments. Nobody *seems* to have a moderate opinion: either, like myself, people find it a masterpiece of its genre or they cannot abide it, and among the hostile there are some, I must confess, for whose literary judgment I have great respect.

In the 21st century Tolkien still has his detractors in the literary establishment, but the attention given to his work by more and more gifted scholars cannot be ignored indefinitely. A leading scholar, Tom Shippey, has argued convincingly for Tolkien's place in the canon of literature.

In *J.R.R. Tolkien: Author of the Century* (2000) Shippey engages in a sophisticated literary debate against Tolkien's detractors, presenting a carefully reasoned and measured defence of his literary greatness. As a philologist who was a successor to Tolkien's Chair at Leeds University, Shippey provides a philological analysis of Tolkien's work. He comments:

> In my opinion (it is not one shared, for instance, by the definitions of the *Oxford English Dictionary*), the essence of philology is, first, the study of historical forms of a language or languages, including dialectical or non-standard forms, and also of related languages.... However, philology is not and should not be confined to language study. The texts in which these old forms of the language survive are often literary works of great power and distinctiveness, and (in the philological view) any literary study which ignores them, which refuses to pay the necessary linguistic toll to be able to read them, is accordingly incomplete and impoverished. Conversely, of course, any study which remains solely linguistic (as was often the case with twentieth century philology) is throwing away its best material and its best argument for existence. In philology, *literary and linguistic study are indissoluble*. They ought to be the same thing.

Tolkien, Shippey points out, believed in this indissolubility.

Though Tolkien's sources are ancient (from early English for example) Shippey points out that Tolkien is a writer belonging squarely to our time, concerned with contemporary themes such as the nature of evil (an "eternal issue" but "terribly re-focussed" in Tolkien's lifetime), cultural relativity, and the "corruptions and continuities of language". Far from being reactionary, Tolkien is at the leading edge in his artistic and intellectual concerns. "The dominant literary mode of the twentieth century," argues Shippey, has been the fantastic.... When the time comes to look back at the [twentieth] century, it seems very likely that future literary historians, detached from the squabbles of our present, will see as its most representative and distinctive works books like J.R.R. Tolkien's *The Lord of the Rings*, and also George Orwell's *Nineteen Eighty-Four* and *Animal Farm*, William Golding's *Lord of the Flies* and *The Inheritors*, Kurt Vonnegut's *Slaughterhouse-Five* and *Cat's Cradle*, Ursula Le Guin's *The Left Hand of Darkness* and *The Dispossessed*, Thomas Pynchon's *The Crying of Lot-49* and *Gravity's Rainbow*.... By the end of the century, even writers deeply committed to the realist novel have often found themselves unable to resist the gravitational pull of the fantastic as a literary mode.

For Shippey, therefore, the continuing appeal of Tolkien cannot be ignored as simply a freak of popular consumption, to be ignored by the well-educated.

Tolkien objected to the reporter's question about what made him tick. This was because he was extremely sensitive to the modern issue of the machine, which dominates *The Lord of the Rings*. Indeed, in a way, the Ring itself is the culmination of the machine, exerting remorseless control over human life and being itself uncontrollable. C.S. Lewis called our present time the "Age of the Machine", a view Tolkien implicitly endorsed in his work. In older times, Lewis believed, the human issue was how to relate to nature, the non-human world. Today's issue is how we relate to the machine that we ourselves have spawned.

Because of his preoccupation with the machine, and for many other reasons, Tolkien is a contemporary writer, rather than a nostalgic sentimentalist. As Shippey points out, he belongs with Orwell and Golding in his endeavour to come to terms with modern global warfare and manifest evil. Even in this endeavour, however, Tolkien avoids the mechanical archetype of the newer being the better (what C.S. Lewis called our "chronological snobbery"). He not only addresses the unprecedented situation of warfare dominated by the new magicians, as he saw them, the scientific technocrats with weapons beyond the reach of the human mind and destructive of humanity (and as real in the trenches of the Somme in World War One as it was in the bombing of Nagasaki). But, even more, Tolkien was concerned with the perennial battle to live virtuously, with honour, sacrifice, courage, seeking fellowship and loving beauty, in a world he saw as radically fallen and broken. In this world malice against the weak and helpless is dreadfully real. Nothing marks the wider and more ancient context of Tolkien's writing than his momentous reversal of the Quest, which in literature is usually for something that represents what is new and desirable to the human heart. In *The Lord of the Rings*, as everyone knows, the Quest is to destroy something that corrupts almost anyone that touches it, offering unfettered power over others. Tolkien's uniqueness in this reversal of the Quest is pointed out by the Polish scholar Tadeusz Andrzej Olszański:

> What Tolkien did in *The Lord of the Rings* was to reverse the old "queste" pattern, or knight's search, thus negating one of the basic dogmas of the European civilisation. The future of Middle-earth is not conditional upon conquering a new thing; it depends on [an] annihilating of what already exists. A solution to any crisis cannot be found—as claimed by Tolkien—in "an escape forward", in conquering and creating newer and newer values and things.[1]

In Tolkien's tale, the meek inherit Middle-earth.

Colin Duriez
November 2003

WORK CITED

J.R.R. Tolkien: *Recepcja Polska*. Edited by Jakub Z. Lichański (Warsaw: Wydawnictwa Uniwersytetu Warszawskiego, 1996, p. 214

CHAPTER ONE

A Career Begins

*Being a cult figure in one's own lifetime I am afraid
is not at all pleasant.... it makes me feel extremely
small and inadequate. But even the nose of a very
modest idol cannot remain entirely untickled by the
sweet smell of incense.*

—Tolkien (Carpenter, ed., *Letters:* 418)

IN THE SUMMER OF 1916, Second Lieutenant J.R.R. Tolkien was
shipped from a training camp in Staffordshire, England, to the
"front," the trenches of Amien, in northern France, for the "Big
Push" against the German army. He was about to be part of the
Battle of the Somme. Its first day, nearly twenty-thousand English
soldiers were killed and sixty-thousand injured advancing on the
German line. Out of the trenches, through poison gas, soldiers
trudged with their guns firing inside the no-man's-land of the several hundred yards separating the English from the Germans, and
they were annihilated by the shells fired back at them.

Just having passed the examination in English Language and
Literature at Oxford with a "First," and newly wed to Edith Bratt,
the girl he had cherished for three years while he was forbidden to
see or even write to her, Tolkien arrived at the front in July 1916.
He fought in the trenches until November. Then he was evacuated

to a hospital at Le Touquet, on the French coast with "pyrexia of unknown origin," trench fever—an infectious disease whose symptoms were sudden fevers, severe headaches, sore muscles, bones, and joints, and skin lesions on the chest and back. He had escaped physical injury while fighting in the trenches, but succumbed to the disease borne by the lice that bred on the men stuck in them. When after a week he showed no sign of improving, he was sent back to England to a hospital in Birmingham. He stayed six weeks before he seemed well enough to travel, in December, with Edith, to the house in which she had lived since their marriage, in the village of Great Hayward in Staffordshire. They enjoyed a pleasant interlude away from the war, even if always aware that Tolkien would ultimately have to return to the danger he had managed to survive the first time. Tolkien seemed to have recuperated. Edith conceived a child, their eldest son, John, who was born November 16, 1917. But the pattern of apparent recovery, reassignment to a base in England for retraining before being sent back to France, and then a resurgence of the fever which kept him from returning to active duty repeated itself for the next year and a half until the end of the war, November 11, 1918. In a letter to him some time during this period Edith teased him, writing, "I should think you ought never to feel tired again for the amount of *Bed* you have had since you came back from France nearly two years ago is enormous." (Carpenter, *Tolkien*: 99)

During this period of recuperation from his five months on the battlefield, Tolkien continued composing the tales of *The Silmarillion*. He had begun writing about a rich and complex fantasy world as an escape inward even while on the battlefield. He used whatever paper he could find, like the back of a sheet outlining the chain of responsibility in his battalion (www.christianitytoday.com), writing "in huts full of blasphemy and smut, or by candle light in bell-tents, even down in dugouts under shell fire". (Carpenter, ed., *Letters*: 78) Back in England, recuperating in hospital he wrote in an inexpensive notebook which he labeled "The Book of Lost Tales" the beginning of what would become *The Silmarillion*. *The Silmarillion* is less well-known than *The Hobbit* or *The Lord of the Rings* but it was seminal to Tolkien, establishing the groundwork for those books. Although it predates *The Hobbit* and *The Lord of the Rings*, Tolkien did not complete it. He worked on it throughout his life, amplifying and revising it, up until 1973, the year of his death. Essentially, *The Silmarillion* is a series of tales, which make up a connected narrative and provide a description and development of the mythology Tolkien was inventing and which became the foundation for his fantasy novels. It was published in 1977 in an edition fashioned from his father's many versions and revisions by Tolkien's youngest son, Christopher.

John Ronald Reuel Tolkien, was born January 3, 1892, in Bloemfontein, Orange Free State, South Africa, where his father, Arthur Reuel Tolkien was the manager of a branch of the Bank of Africa. Arthur Tolkien had come to Bloemfontein from Birmingham. In England, his family had manufactured Tolkien Pianos until the firm went bankrupt. Arthur became a clerk in Lloyds Bank in the Birmingham office. In Birmingham, too, he met Mabel Suffield. Like Arthur's father, her father had once been prosperous. He had owned a drapery business until he, too, went bankrupt and became a commercial traveler—a traveling salesman—for *Jeyes Disinfectant.* After she turned eighteen Arthur proposed marriage to Mabel. Her father thought her too young and would not allow a formal betrothal until two years had passed. In the meantime, the sundered lovers communicated in secret by letter. Arthur determined that real advancement was not likely in Birmingham and set out for South Africa. Mabel was to follow when he could support her. Arthur Tolkien succeeded; he was earning an adequate income, and the bank provided a house for them. In March, 1891, now with her father's blessing, Mabel embarked on the steamer *Robin Castle* to join him. On April 16, 1891, they were married in the Anglican Cathedral in Cape Town. She was twenty-one and he was thirty-four. Ten months later J.R.R. Tolkien, called Ronald by his family, was born.

Bloemfontein was hardly a city. It was like a frontier town in a Western movie. An oasis in desert country, it was windy, dusty and being developed. It offered little but employment for Arthur and domesticity for Mabel. The trees which had been planted by the settlers were still young. It was too hot in the summer and too cold in the winter. It was, politically and culturally, a part of the Orange Free State, a Dutch enclave in a country divided between Dutch and British administrations, which soon would be warring with each other in the Boer War. Mabel did not like it in Africa nor did she approve the Boer exploitation of the majority African population. Tolkien recalled her attitude in a wartime letter to his son Christopher, who was stationed in South Africa during the Second World War. His words are cryptic because he is weaving around the military censorship of wartime mail:

> As for what you say or hint of "local" conditions: I knew of them.... I used to hear them discussed by my mother.... The treatment of colour nearly always horrifies anyone going out from Britain, & not only in South Africa. Unfort. [unfortunately] not many retain that generous sentiment for long.
>
> (Carpenter, ed., *Letters:* 73)

In a family photograph taken in November 1892, two African servants are included in the family grouping with Arthur, Mabel, and the baby Ronald, who is being held by his nurse. They look more like members of the family than servants. Isak, the house boy, in fact, is wearing the same style straw hat as Arthur. Once, after Isak had taken the baby Ronald, without having asked the Tolkiens' permission, proudly to show him to his own family, Arthur and Mabel were upset, but Isak was not fired. (Carpenter, *Tolkien:* 13)

Two years after Tolkien, his brother Hilary was born. They grew up in nature, close to the earth, exposed to its perils. There were animals, some dangerous, all around them. Wolves, wild dogs and jackals menaced the flocks. In the tall grass of the Tolkien's garden lurked snakes and tarantulas. Tolkien recalled, "I was nearly bitten by snakes and I was stung by a tarantula, I believe. In my garden. All I can remember is a very hot day, long, dead grass, and running. I don't even remember screaming." (Grotta-Kurska: 15) His African nurse sucked the venom from his foot and saved his life. The brothers also watched their father plant a grove of cypress, fir and cedar trees, and Tolkien developed a love of trees and of climbing them. The heat, however, affected him badly, and he was often ill. (Carpenter, *Tolkien*: 14)

Despite visits from England from her sister, whose husband was traveling in South Africa on business, Mabel tried to convince her husband to take a trip to England because the climate did not agree with her or her son, and also because she was homesick. He was reluctant. Indeed, he had written to his father, "I think I shall do well in this country and do not think I should settle down well in England again for a permanency," (Carpenter, *Tolkien*: 15) and he was studying Dutch, the language in which business was conducted in Bloemfontein.

When she learned she was pregnant again, Mabel, too, had to put off thoughts of making a trip. But in April, 1895, Mabel and the two boys took the S.S *Guelph* from South Africa back to England, expecting it to be only for a visit. Arthur felt he was unable to leave his work at the bank. Their departure was, however, to be permanent. In November, she learned that Arthur had come down with rheumatic fever. As Mabel was preparing early in 1896 for the trip back to care for him she received a telegram that Arthur had died. He was buried in the Anglican graveyard in Bloemfontein. It was a devastating loss to the family. It is clear that he was an important and loved figure for his wife and for his son. The following letter which the four year old Ronald Tolkien sent him—he dictated it to his nurse who wrote it down—in anticipation of the return trip, a letter his father never got to see, attests to that:

My dear Daddy,

I am so glad I am coming back to see you it is such a long time we came away from you I hope the ship will bring us all back to you Mamie and Baby and me. I know you will be so glad to have a letter from your little Ronald it is such a long time since I wrote to you ... Mamie says you will not know Baby or me we have got such big men we have got such a lot of Christmas presents to show you.... Hilary sends lots of love and kisses and so does your loving

Ronald.

(Carpenter, *Tolkien:* 16)

During their visit to England, Mabel and the children stayed in the small, family house on King's Heath in Birmingham with her parents, her sister Jane, her brother William and a lodger. After her husband's death, Mabel Tolkien knew she could not stay on with her parents permanently, and she began to search for a place to live with the children. She got thirty shillings a week from the investment Arthur had made in the Bonanza Mines. (Large amounts of gold, indeed, were being discovered in South Africa.) It wasn't enough, and was supplemented by her family.

She found a semi-detached brick cottage at 5 Gracewell in Sarehole, a hamlet about a mile south of Birmingham. It was part of the English countryside, located among meadows, a broad stream, a mill where wheat had been ground, and a sand pit encircled by trees. It served as the model for the "Shire" in *The Hobbit* and *The Lord of the Rings*. For Ronald and Hilary it was the setting for adventure, a landscape for venturing into and exploring. A steam engine had been installed to power the mill when the river was low, and rather than wheat, the mill now ground bones for the production of fertilizer. There were two millers, father and son. To the boys they were perfect mean storybook characters who often chased and threatened them when they hung around watching the mill-work. Ronald called the father "the Black Ogre"—he had a long black beard. The son, the White Ogre, was covered with the blanched dust of the pulverized bones. In his old age, Tolkien's brother, Hilary, recalled their childhood:

> We spent lovely summers just picking flowers and trespassing.... [I]n order to get to the place where we used to blackberry (called the Dell) we had to go through the white [ogre's] land, and he didn't like us very much because the path was narrow through the field and we traipsed off after corn cockles and other pretty things. My mother got us lunch to have in this lovely place, but when she arrived she made a deep voice and we both ran.
>
> (Carpenter, *Tolkien:* 21)

Ronald and Hilary, at first, were not accepted by the neighborhood children. Mabel kept their curly hair long and dressed them in finery, "short black velvet coats and knee-length trousers, large round hats with draw strings, frilly white satin shirts with wide collars, and huge red bow ribbons loosely tied at the neck." Tolkien later reported that "the village children rather despised me because my mother liked me to be pretty."(Grotta-Kurska: 17)

Even in his infancy, she had doted on his appearance, and wrote to her mother-in-law with prescience she could not know she was showing, "Baby does look such a fairy when he's *very* much dressed-up in white frills and white shoes. When he's *un*dressed I think he looks more of an elf still. (Carpenter, *Tolkien*: 14) Tolkien apparently made an effort most of his adult life not "to be pretty," choosing rather colorless tweeds. Towards the end of his life, however, and when the success of his books allowed him to afford them, he liked to wear and even point out that he did wear, colorful velvet vests. Despite his mother's taste when he was a child, he finally did make friends with the neighborhood children and picked up the Warwickshire dialect and the local vocabulary.

Mabel Tolkien was a highly accomplished woman of strong will and determination. She taught Ronald to read by four, and soon after, to cultivate fine penmanship. She also began teaching him Latin, which he liked very much, and French, which he did not. Apart from learning the meaning of Latin words, he apparently liked their sound and shape. He didn't take to the piano, but he was good at drawing. Mabel went with the children on walks and taught them botany. Tolkien was very fond of trees. He drew them, climbed them, and talked to them. He continued communing with trees until old age.

Among the books Mabel gave him to read, he did not like Robert Louis Stevenson's *Treasure Island,* nor did he like Hans Christian Andersen's stories, nor *The Pied Piper.* He did like *Alice in Wonderland* and a series of books by George MacDonald, the "Curdie" books, better. They "were set in a remote kingdom where misshapen and malevolent goblins lurked beneath the mountains." (Carpenter, *Tolkien*: 22) He also liked the Arthurian stories. His favorite story, however, was the tale of Sigurd who slew Fafnir, a dragon, in Andrew Lang's *Red Fairy Book.* About his fascination for dragons and their power over his imagination,

Tolkien later wrote:

> I desired dragons with a profound desire. Of course, I in my timid body did not wish to have them in the neighborhood. But the world that contained even the imagination of Fafnir was richer and more beautiful, at whatever cost of peril.
>
> (Carpenter, *Tolkien:* 22-3)

When he was seven he tried to write a story himself about a dragon:

> I remember nothing about it except a philological fact. My mother said nothing about the dragon, but pointed out that one could not say "a green great dragon," but had to say "a great green dragon." I wondered why, and still do. The fact that I remember this is possibly significant, as I do not think I ever tried to write a story again for many years, and was taken up with language.
>
> (Carpenter, *Tolkien:* 23)

CHAPTER TWO

Boyhood

Come sing ye light fairy things tripping so gay,
Like visions, like glinting reflections of joy
All fashion'd of radiance, careless of grief,
O'er this green and brown carpet; nor hasten away.
O! come to me! dance for me! Sprites of the wood,
O! come to me! Sing to me once ere ye fade!
—Tolkien, "Wood-sunshine," 1910.

WHEN HENRY VIII DEFIED EXCOMMUNICATION and proclaimed his independence from papal authority in 1534, after having divorced Catherine of Aragon and married Anne Boleyn, he established an English Church independent of the Roman Catholic Church, with himself at its head. Those Catholics, like Sir Thomas More, who opposed him, Henry sent to the Tower of London and had beheaded. Under the reign of Henry's son Edward VI and of Edward Seymour, the Lord Protector—the new king was ten years old—Protestantism was established in England and, in 1549, the Anglican Book of Common Prayer was introduced. Edward died of tuberculosis in 1553, and his half sister, Mary, reigned for five years. During her reign she restored Catholicism to England, reinstated the Mass, returned to Rome Church lands Henry had confiscated, married Philip of Spain, staunchly Roman Catholic, and was given the name Bloody Mary for her persecution of Protestants. She died in 1558 and Elizabeth I, her half-sister began her famous reign and restored Protestantism, making the Church of England the Established Church in 1559. Under Elizabeth the practice of Catholicism was outlawed and Catholics were persecuted. Fierce animosity, generally less bloody, but not always, as in the case of Ireland, has existed historically ever since between the Protestant and the Roman Catholic Churches, an animosity intensified by the place of the two faiths in English social, economic, and political conflicts.

Tolkien's parents were Anglican, but after the death of her husband, Mabel Tolkien was drawn to the Catholic faith and, with her sister May, took instruction in Catholicism at St. Anne's, a church located in the slums of Birmingham. In June of 1900, the sisters were received into the Roman Catholic faith. Their family was furious. Their father had been raised a Methodist and had become a Unitarian. May's husband, Walter, a respectable Anglican forbade her to enter a Catholic Church. She obeyed him. Walter also had been giving financial assistance to Mabel since Arthur Tolkien's death. She defied his wishes and held to her faith, and he disowned her. The strain of family hostility and the resulting increase in financial hardship seriously affected Mabel's health, but did not break her faith nor her determination to instill the Catholic faith in her sons.

Most of Arthur's relatives were as offended by Mabel's conversion as her own family was, but not everyone. A Tolkien uncle paid the tuition for Ronald's schooling at King Edward's after he passed the entrance examination in 1900, after having failed it the year before. King Edward VI Grammar School was the school his father had gone to. It was in a grand Victorian building, soot blackened and overcrowded, but it was the best school in Birmingham. It was located in the center of the city, and Ronald had to walk most of the way—four miles—from Sarehole to school. His mother could not afford the train fare and the Birmingham trams did not go as far as Sarehole. Mabel, in consequence, gave up the openness of the countryside for a rented house in Mosley—a suburb of the city on the tram line. It was near an urban district, where trams and factory smokestacks silhouetted the industrial community. Tolkien did not like the change from the Warwickshire countryside, where, he later wrote, the four years he had spent there were the "most formative part of my life." But he liked school, even though he was frequently absent because of poor health.

They did not stay long in their house because it was condemned so that a fire station could be built. They moved to a row house near King's Heath Station and not far from a coal-yard. They could hear the noise of trains and trucks. Tolkien played on the grassy slopes near the rail-yard and was fascinated by the words written in Welsh, the place names on the coal trucks: *Nantyglo, Senghenydd, Blaen-Rhondda, Penrhiwceiber,* and *Tredegar.* (Carpenter, *Tolkien:* 26)

Mabel did not like the house, the neighborhood or the nearby church, a new Roman Catholic Church, St. Dunstan's. On a Sunday walk with the boys she came upon the Birmingham Oratory, a Roman Catholic Church and the residence of a community of priests who cared for it. The Grammar School of St. Philip was also attached to the Oratory. Unlike King Edward's, which was Protestant, it was a Catholic school. The Birmingham Oratory had been established by John Henry Newman in 1849, soon after he had converted to Catholicism and he had lived there until his death in 1890. Newman rose to eminence in the Church becoming a cardinal and was the author of *The Idea of the University* and the *Apologia pro vita sua.* (James Joyce regarded him as among the greatest prose writers in English.) In 1902, Mabel rented the house next door to the Oratory school. That September, Tolkien and his brother began to attend St. Philip's. (Carpenter, *Tolkien:* 26)

It was a much better life for them than they had been leading despite the fact that both boys were sick with a variety of the childhood diseases, taxing their mother sorely. They had the good fortune to meet Father Francis Xavier Morgan, a member of the community and their parish priest. He was forty-three in 1902. He had been a member of the community since 1875, during Cardinal Newman's last years. He had served under Newman and been his friend. He also became a good friend to Mabel Tolkien and her family, and Tolkien thought of him as his "second father." (Carpenter, ed., *Letters*: 416) In 1941, Tolkien wrote to his son Michael that Father Francis "had been a father to me, more than most real fathers, but without any obligation." (Carpenter, ed., *Letters*: 55) Father Francis was of Welsh and Anglo-Spanish extraction. Humphrey Carpenter, Tolkien's authorized biographer, writes that

> he was not a man of great intellect, but he had an immense fund of kindness and humor and a flamboyance that was often attributed to his Spanish connections.... he was a very noisy man, loud and affectionate, embarrassing to small children at first but hugely lovable when they got to know him.
>
> (Carpenter, *Tolkien*: 27)

Even though St. Philip's grammar school was near their home, cheaper than King Edward's, and a Catholic school, it could not provide the kind of education Tolkien got at King Edward's. Mabel took him out of St. Philip's and taught him herself, as she had done before he had entered King Edward's. After a few months of her schooling, Tolkien won a Foundation Scholarship and returned to King Edward VI in the autumn of 1903. Although attending a Protestant school was something of an anomaly, Tolkien, throughout his life, considered it a beneficial anomaly. In 1968, he wrote to Michael:

> I had the advantage of a (then) first rate school and that of a "good Catholic home"—"in excelsis": virtually a junior inmate of the Oratory house, which contained many learned fathers.... Observance of religion was strict. Hilary and I were supposed to, and usually did, serve Mass before getting on our bikes to go to school in New Street. So I grew up in a two front state, symbolized by the Oration Italian pronunciation of Latin, and the strictly "philological" pronunciation at that time introduced into our Cambridge dominated school....
>
> (Carpenter, ed., *Letters*: 395)

As important as the Warwickshire countryside was to his development, so the King Edward School was, too. The countryside opened for him the resources of nature and the experience of living in and finding pleasure in the natural world. School opened to him the life of the mind and the puzzles of the intellect. The two forces worked equally strongly and cooperatively in him, inculcating in him a devotion to and an ease with regard to both nature and culture. At school, Tolkien was fascinated by language as he had been under his mother's instruction. He was excited by the otherness of Greek, by its distance from his daily experience:

> The fluidity of Greek, punctuated by hardness, and with its surface glitter captivated me. But part of the attraction was antiquity and alien remoteness (from me); it did not touch home.
>
> (Carpenter, *Tolkien:* 27)

He studied literature, too, and discovered his dislike of Shakespeare, epitomized by his

> bitter disappointment and disgust from schooldays with the shabby use made in Shakespeare of the coming of "Great Birnham Wood to high Dunsinane hill": I longed to devise a setting by which the trees might really march to war.
>
> (Carpenter, *Tolkien:* 28)

This is precisely the sort of thing he did go on to write in *The Hobbit, The Lord of the Rings* and *The Silmarillion,* where the heroic animation of opposing forces in nature and the soul rather than the irony of experience is the central concern. But Tolkien liked reading Chaucer and he liked hearing his teacher recite *The Canterbury Tales* using Middle English pronunciation.

In December, 1903, Mabel described their situation in a Christmas letter to her mother-in-law, Arthur's mother. It shows her as a mother actively involved in forming her elder son. (She had written in an earlier letter that Hilary, her younger, was "dreamy and slow at writing" despite her efforts.) But she was also ill and strained to the limits of her strength:

(…) I haven't been out for almost a *month*—not even to The Oratory!—but the nasty wet muggy weather is making me better and since Ronald broke up I have been able to rest in the mornings. I keep having whole weeks of utter sleeplessness, which added to the internal cold and sickness have made it almost impossible to go on.

(Carpenter, *Tolkien:* 28)

A few months later, in April 1904, Mabel Tolkien was hospitalized with diabetes. Ronald was sent to live with her parents and Hilary to her sister. In June, Mabel had recovered sufficiently to be released from the hospital. Father Francis Morgan arranged for her to have a bedroom and a sitting room in the cottage of the postman and his wife, Mr. and Mrs. Till, in Rednal, near Birmingham. The cottage was on the grounds of a house which Cardinal Newman had built as a retreat for the members of the Oratory community. Mrs. Till cooked for them, too and the boys thrived. They were back in the country, it was summer, and they had the freedom of the countryside. In a post-card to Arthur's mother, Mabel wrote:

Boys look *ridiculously* well compared to the weak white ghosts that met me on train 4 weeks ago!!! Hilary has got tweed suit and his first Etons today! And looks *immense.*—We've had perfect weather. Boys will write first wet day but what with Bilberry-gathering—Tea in Hay—Kite-flying with Fr. Francis—sketching—Tree Climbing—they've never enjoyed a holiday so much.

In addition, Father Francis had a dog and often sat

on the ivy-covered veranda of the Oratory house smoking a large cherrywood pipe; "the more remarkable," Ronald recalled, "since he never smoked except there. Possibly my own later addiction to the Pipe derives from this.

(Carpenter, *Tolkien:* 30)

Ronald returned to King Edward's in September and the family stayed on in the cottage until November when Mabel died on the fourteenth, six days after going into a diabetic coma. Ronald was twelve. The loss of his mother was as profound as his love and esteem for her. In a letter to his son Michael, sixty-eight years later, in 1972, about a year and a half before his own death, Tolkien recalled, "when I was not yet thirteen after the death of my mother," "vainly waving a hand at the sky saying 'it is so empty and cold.'" He was "trying to tell [his first cousin] Marjorie Incledon how he felt "like a castaway left on a barren island under a heedless sky after the loss of a great ship." (Carpenter, ed., *Letters*: 416) To an important degree his love for and his devotion to the Catholic faith were aspects or extensions of his love for and devotion to his mother. He wrote of her on several occasions in his letters. To his son, Michael, when he was being trained as a soldier at the Royal Military College at Sandhurst in 1941, Tolkien wrote:

> [y]our grandmother, to whom you owe so much…was a gifted lady of great beauty and wit, greatly stricken by God with grief and suffering, who died in youth (at 34) of a disease hastened by perse-cution of her faith.
>
> (Carpenter, ed., *Letters:* 54)

In 1965, he wrote to Michael, apparently when Michael was having a crisis of faith:

> When I think of my mother's death (younger than Prisca [his daughter, Priscilla]) worn out with persecution, poverty, and, largely consequent, disease, in the effort to hand on to us small boys the Faith, and remember the tiny bedroom she shared with us in rented rooms in a postman's cottage at Rednal, where she died alone, too ill for viaticum, I find it very hard and bitter, when my children stray away [from the Catholic Faith].
>
> (Carpenter, ed., *Letters:* 353-4)

To a pair of reporters who had interviewed him in 1967, he wrote,

> My interest in languages was derived solely from my mother…. She knew German, and gave me my first lessons in it. She was also

interested in etymology, and aroused my interest in this; and also in alphabets and handwriting…. Two years before her death I had with her sole tuition (except in geometry which I was taught by her sister) gained a scholarship to King Edward VI School in Birmingham.

(Carpenter, ed., *Letters:* 377)

After their mother's death, Father Francis was wary of letting Ronald and Hilary live with any of Mabel's family, fearing the boys would be sent to a Protestant boarding school and drawn away from the Catholic faith. One of Mabel's aunts, Beatrice Suffield, however, was indifferent to religion and would not, therefore, challenge their faith. Farther Francis arranged for them to live with her. She dispatched her duty with coldness. Young Ronald, for example, saw her burn his mother's papers and letters in the grate. She apparently felt they were neither of use nor of interest to anyone. (Carpenter, *Tolkien:* 33) She lived not far from the Oratory, however, and Ronald and Hilary virtually lived there. Mornings, before school, they served the mass and had their breakfast with Father Francis and then walked from the Oratory or took a horse drawn bus or rode their bicycles to King Edward's School.

DURING THE YEARS that Tolkien spent at King Edward's, following his mother's death, he became attached to all the things which would be significant to him throughout his life, and, four years after his beloved mother's death, he met the young woman he would marry.

In school, he encountered inspiring teachers able to guide his enthusiasms. He found Anglo-Saxon and the epic Old English poem *Beowulf.* A teacher gave him a *Primer of the Gothic Language,* "an East Germanic language, in which [the] only [surviving] document of any length is a sixth-century … Bible." (Rogers, D. and I. Rogers: 42) He learned Gothic and could speak and write it fluently. He had already begun inventing his own language. With his cousins Marjorie and Mary Incledon, he developed "Animalic," where animal names replaced other words, so that "'*Dog nightingale woodpecker forty*" meant 'You are an ass.'" "Animalic" developed into the much more sophisticated "Nevbosh," ("New Nonsense,") in which Ronald and Mary made up limericks like this one:

Dar fys ma vel co palt "Hoc
Pys go iskili far maino woc?
Pro si go fys do roc de
D cat ym maino bocte
De volt fact soc ma taimful gyroc!"
(There was an old man who said, How
Can I possibly carry a cow?
For if I were to ask it
To get in my basket
It would make such a terrible row!")

(Carpenter, *Tolkien:* 36)

Now at King Edward's he continued to work in earnest at constructing words, alphabets, languages, grammars, and the cultures in which they might have developed. It was an interest and a practice that lay at the heart of his work as the author of his epic romances, *The Hobbit, The Lord of the Rings* and *The Silmarillion.*

At King Edward's, too, he was thrown into contact with young men of equally lively brilliance and interests as his. A group of them began having tea in the library, and they called their gatherings meetings of the Tea Club, which became "T.C". Sometimes they went to Barrow's Stores—which became "B.S."—and had tea there. They called themselves the T.C.B.S.: The Tea Club and Barrovian Society. They forged deep friendships and shared their hopes, ideals, and expectations of future success in their fields. They gave each other confidence, they made each other feel special, and they helped each other on with their work, listening to it, appreciating it, and encouraging it. In this way the T.C.B.S. was the precursor to the *Inklings,* the vital circle of friends formed at Oxford in the 1930s around Tolkien and C. S. Lewis.

There were four principal members of the T.C.B.S. at King Edward's: Tolkien was one; Christopher Wiseman, a mathematician, musician, and composer was another. R.Q. Gilson, the son of the school's headmaster, was interested in drawing and designing. His expertise included Renaissance painting and the Eighteenth Century. Geoffrey Bache Smith was younger than the others and he was not a classicist as they were. His field was English Literature and Poetry. He was himself well-regarded as a poet, and in that respect was particularly in tune with and important to Tolkien, who had begun writing verse himself, in which the English countryside and its animating spirits were already present both as ambience and subject. This is demonstrated in his poem, "Woodsunshine," quoted at the beginning of this chapter.

Gilson and Smith were killed in 1916 in the Battle of the Somme, the same disastrous battle from which Tolkien was evacuated sick after five months in the trenches. The death of these two signaled the death of the youthful bright vision of T.C.B.S. It left a great darkness for Tolkien to fill as much as he could with his own light. Carrying on under such painful circumstances is altogether in the English manner of remaining active, bearing, and making the best of adversity, and it is true to the Roman Catholic understanding that bearing the pain of the world is inevitable since the world—although God's—is a fallen world. Tolkien had already had a lesson in such carrying on with the death of his mother. But with the brightness of brilliant youth, undeterred yet by the visible darkness of war, and with a circle of friends as full of life as himself, Tolkien developed at school both his life-long pursuits: writing epic faery myth and doing philology.

During the summer vacation of 1908, Father Francis took the boys to Lyme Regis, where Tolkien sketched the scenery on wet days and explored the shore line and the cliffs nearby. His biographer, Humphrey Carpenter, reports that once he found a prehistoric jawbone there and pretended it was a dragon's. When Father Francis learned that the boys were not happy at their Aunt Beatrice's cold and gloomy house, he found them lodging with Mrs. Faulkner, a woman who lived behind the Oratory and who held "musical evenings," which some of the priests attended. In addition to her husband, a wine merchant, her daughter, and the maid, another lodger, beside Ronald and Hilary, lived in her house.

Edith Bratt was nineteen, three years older than Tolkien. She, too, was an orphan but had never known her father. Her parents had not been married, but her mother did keep a photograph of him. When she died, Edith was sent to boarding school. She had shown real talent as a pianist, and she was trained at school to be either a piano teacher or, perhaps, a concert pianist. Her guardian was the family solicitor who found her the lodgings with Mrs. Faulkner after boarding school, but did nothing to foster either aspects of her career. There was no pressing need in his mind for her to work since she had a small inheritance large enough to keep her. Mrs. Faulkner also, despite her musical evenings, thwarted Edith's development. Although glad to have Edith accompany singers at her gatherings, Mrs. Faulkner was intolerant of any real practicing Edith would attempt during the day and interrupted her when she got down to scales. Circumstances, not her lack of talent, guaranteed that Edith had no prospect of a concert career or a career as a piano teacher ahead of her. To say that Edith lived in an age when it was common and culturally acceptable for most girls and women to be defined as having less important interests than boys and men is certainly true. That did not, however, make it easier for the girls and women who lived through it and even accepted (or resigned themselves to) it. Edith suffered from the effects of sexually defined inferiority throughout her life, including in her marriage. Tolkien's views of women, while not reactionary, nevertheless, conformed to the views of his era, which simultaneously elevated and subordinated women.

When Ronald and Hilary moved in to Mrs. Faulkner's house, Edith and the boys became good friends. The brothers would sneak down to her room at night and the three would share the scraps of food which Edith had cribbed from the kitchen. They also established a pulley system outside the house between their windows to send food up and down. Edith and Ronald took walks by themselves and drank tea in tea-rooms together. In the summer of 1909, he was seventeen, she twenty, they fell in love. Years later, in a letter to Edith he remembered:

my first kiss to you and your first kiss to me (which was almost

accidental)—and our goodnights when sometimes you were in
your little white nightgown, and our absurd long window talks;
and how we watched the sun come up over town through the mist
and Big Ben toll hour after hour, and the moths almost used to
frighten you away—and our whistle-call—and our cycle rides—
and the fire talks—and the three great kisses.

(Carpenter, Tolkien: 40)

Tolkien was active in all aspects of school life at King Edward.
He joined the Debating Society and gave speeches supporting
women's suffrage, deploring the Norman invasion of England in
1066, condemning "the influx of polysyllabic barbarities which
ousted the more honest if humbler native words," and savaging
Shakespeare. According to a review of his speech in the school
magazine, the young Tolkien "poured a sudden flood of unquali-
fied abuse upon Shakespeare, upon his filthy birthplace, his
squalid surroundings, and his sordid character." (Carpenter,
Tolkien: 40) Of his ferocious playing on the Rugby field despite his
light weight, Tolkien wrote, "Having the romantic upbringing, I
made a boy-and-girl affair serious, and made it a source of effort.
Naturally rather a physical coward, I passed from a despised rabbit
on a house second-team to school colours in two seasons." (Carpenter, ed., *Letters:* 52) The relationship with Edith was serious
and it was secret, and it was facilitated by their easy and natural
contact with each other. As lodgers in the same home, they could
often be together.

In the fall of 1909, however, they wanted to go out together,
too. They arranged to meet secretly. "We thought," Tolkien
wrote, "we had managed things very cleverly. Edith had ridden
off on her bicycle nominally to visit her cousin.... After an
interval, I rode off." (Carpenter, *Tolkien:* 41) They spent the day
on the hills and then went down to Rednal Village for tea, and
then home separately. A chain of gossip, however, beginning with
the proprietress of the tea-shop, linking to the caretaker of the
Oratory House, then to the cook there, finally was completed
when the cook told Father Francis. Father Francis forbade Ronald
to continue seeing Edith, and he arranged for the boys to live

elsewhere. It was in the midst of this melodrama that Tolkien failed to make Oxford. At a low ebb, Tolkien began a diary. On New Year's Day, 1910, he wrote: "Depressed and as much in the dark as ever. God help me. Feel weak and weary." (Carpenter, *Tolkien*: 42) He also, however, realized that he had another try for Oxford, and, as he had done with his mother when he failed to make King Edward's on his first try, he applied himself. The next year he succeeded.

He also did not break contact with Edith. They met secretly once and took the train out to the country to spend the afternoon, and they bought each other gifts. She bought him a pen for his eighteenth birthday. He bought her a wristwatch for her twenty-first. They went to a shop and had tea together. Edith told him she was going to Cheltenham to live with an aged couple. But they were seen. Father Francis forbade him even to write to her, and warned that if he were not obeyed he would withdraw his support. This stricture would be in place for three years, until Tolkien was twenty-one. Father Francis did allow Tolkien to see Edith off and tell her then. Tolkien managed to see her before that:

> Last night prayed would see E. by accident. Prayer answered. Saw her at 12.55 at Prince of Wales. Told her I could not write and arranged to see her off on Thursday fortnight. Happier but so much long to see her just once to cheer her up. Cannot think of anything else.

On February 21, "I saw a dejected little figure sloshing along in a mac and tweed hat and could not resist crossing and saying a word of love and cheerfulness. This cheered me up a little. Prayed and thought hard." Two days later, this was his diary entry: "I met her coming from the Cathedral to pray for me." (Carpenter, *Tolkien*: 41) These meetings were also seen and reported to Father Francis. Tolkien wrote in his diary on February 26:

> had a dreadful letter from Fr. F. saying I had been seen with a girl again, calling it evil and foolish. Threatening to cut short my university career if I did not stop. Means I cannot see E. Nor write at

all. God help me. Saw E. at midday but would not be with her. I owe all to Fr. F. and so must obey.

(Carpenter, Tolkien: 43)

Tolkien, however, did not give Edith up. They were in love, and they promised to wait three years until he was twenty-one. It was a situation very similar to the one Tolkien's parents had faced before their marriage, when his father was made to wait two years before he could become engaged to his mother.

CHAPTER THREE

Internal Resources

Earendel sprang up from Ocean's cup
In the gloom of the mid world's rim:
From the door of Night as a ray of light
Leapt over the twilight brim,
And launching his bark like a silver spark
From the golden fading sand
Down the sunlit breath of Day's fiery death
He sped from Westerland.
—Tolkien, Opening Lines of "The Voyage of
Earendel the Evening Star," 1914.

DESPITE THE EMOTIONAL TURMOIL he endured because of his romance with Edith, and despite the fact that it at first effected his ability to work and to concentrate, Tolkien's last year at King Edward was filled with study, extra-curricular activity, and friendships. His powers were reaching their fullness. He worked hard preparing for the entrance and scholarship exam to Oxford, and after failing it the year before, won an Exhibition Scholarship, not the best he could have done, worth sixty pounds a year. That amount was not enough by itself but it was supplemented by a scholarship from King Edward's and by assistance from Father Francis—who had family money of his own.

Tolkien's expertise in philology had become impressive. He delivered a lecture to the First Class at King Edward's on "The Modern Languages of Europe—Derivations and Capabilities," which he read over three successive hours without finishing. When, during one of the school debates, one which was traditionally done in Latin, he was assigned the role of a Greek Ambassador to the Roman Senate, he spoke his part in Greek. In another, when he was playing a barbarian envoy, he delivered his part in Gothic. But he was not only intellectually lively. He was active in many sports. He broke his nose and cut his tongue playing rugby. Tolkien attributed his life long speech impediment, which often made him hard to understand, to his tongue injury. When his son Michael, away at the Oratory School in Berkshire wrote with disappointment after he failed to make the rugby team, Tolkien offered fatherly encouragement and consolation. He recalled, writing to his son, that he too failed to make the team on the first try, but considering all the injuries he sustained, he was happy Michael remained uninjured even at the cost of not making the team. (Carpenter, ed., *Letters*: 22)

Those who knew Tolkien—his biographer, Humphrey Carpenter reports—testified to the fact that he read poetry with grace and clarity. These performances indicate his diction could be comprehensible and his articulation clear. Indistinctness of speech, when it did occur—from reports by students and colleagues, it was frequent and persisted throughout his life—was probably a result of the rush and tumble of his thought overwhelming his verbal ability rather than of a physical deformation. It seems likely, too, that it was a mark of his inward absorption with his own mental universe. Writing to Michael, in 1968, Tolkien says of it:

> My "friends" among dons were chiefly pleased to tell me that I spoke too fast and might have been interesting if I could be heard. True often: due in part to having too much to say in too little time, in larger part to diffidence, which such comments increased.
>
> (Carpenter, ed., *Letters:* 396)

C. S. Lewis, an Oxford colleague and the foremost of his friends wrote of Tolkien:

...you may not be able to hear what he says. He is a bad lecturer. All the same I advise you to go. If you do, arrive early, sit near the front and pay particular attention to the extempore remarks and comments he often makes. These are usually the best things in the lecture. In fact one could call him an inspired speaker of footnotes.

(Birzer, 4)

Tolkien himself often referred to and joked about his impediment. To an interviewer from the American Library Association who told him, "I do appreciate your coming up from Oxford so that I might record you Professor Tolkien, but I can't understand a word you say," Tolkien responded, "A friend of mine tells me I talk in shorthand and then smudge it." In response to an invitation to deliver a lecture in the United States, Tolkien remarked "I should not, of course, object to lecturing several times. I am quite hardened by it, and even enjoy it—more than my audience." (Birzer, 3) An anecdote about a train trip back to Oxford after lecturing on *Sir Gawain and the Green Knight* in Glasgow, in 1953, reveals something about both his speech and his character:

> I traveled all the way from Motherwell to Wolverhampton with a Scotch mother and a wee lassie, whom I rescued from standing in the corridor of a packed train, and they were allowed to go "first" without payment since I told the inspector I welcomed their company. My reward was to be informed ere we parted that (while I was at lunch) the wee lassie had declared: "I like him but I canna understand a word he says." To which I could only lamely reply that the latter was universal but the former not so usual.
>
> (Carpenter, *Tolkien:* 127)

He was a habitual pipe smoker, too, and he often spoke sucking on a pipe stuck between his teeth.

At King Edward's Tolkien continued inventing languages, studying Norse Sagas, and he discovered the *Kalevala*, or *Land of the Heroes*, an epic poem recounting Finnish mythology. He first read a translation, but then sought out a copy of the original and taught himself to read it in Finnish. During his last term, he played

Hermes in Aristophanes' play, *Peace*. Later, Tolkien described his spirit at this time with an anecdote about his high jinx:

> The school-porter was sent by waiting relatives to find me. He reported that my appearance might be delayed. "Just now," he said, "he's the life and soul of the party." Tactful. In fact, having just taken part in a Greek play, I was clad in a himation and sandals, and was giving what I thought a fair imitation of a frenzied Bacchic dance.
>
> (Carpenter, *Tolkien:* 49)

During the summer of 1911, in the interval between leaving King Edward and beginning at Oxford, Tolkien traveled to Switzerland in a group of a dozen people including his brother Hilary. The excursion was organized by the family on whose farm Hilary was working. Hilary had by this time left school after having chosen to make agriculture his career. It was a great adventure, fraught with excitement and risk, as they hiked through the mountains. (Carpenter, ed., *Letters:* 391-93)

Towards the end of his sojourn in Switzerland, Tolkien bought several picture postcards, among them a reproduction of a painting by a German painter, J. Madelener, called *Der Berggesist,* the mountain spirit. An old man with a white beard, wearing a wide-brimmed hat and a long cloak, sits under a pine tree. He is talking to a white fawn, which is nuzzling its maw in his open palms. His expression is a mixture of humor and compassion. On the paper folder inside which Tolkien kept the picture, he wrote "Origin of Gandalf," the wizard in *The Hobbit* and *The Lord of the Rings*. The experience of climbing a mountain beginning to come loose under one's feet and rolling its boulders is also the model for several such episodes in both works, the first occurring in Chapter IV of *The Hobbit,* "Over Hill and Under Hill," when "[b]oulders ... at times came galloping down the mountain-sides, let loose by mid-day sun upon the snow, and passed among them (which was lucky), or over their heads (which was alarming). (*The Hobbit:* 50)

In the autumn of 1911, Tolkien arrived at Oxford in a motor car driven by R. W. Reynolds, the teacher at King Edward who

had kindled his enthusiasm for poetry. Tolkien's view of himself
and the world did not change during his time at Oxford, nor was
it challenged as it was fighting in the trenches of France. Oxford
was a grander version of King Edward's. The same skills that he
cultivated there, he continued to develop at Oxford, and they
served him well. What was new to him was the climate of class distinction at Oxford. Tolkien himself was a relatively poor young
man and an orphan. His schoolfellows at King Edward mostly
were boys from working class families whose distinction was their
brilliance. Oxford University, during the first decades of the twentieth century, was essentially the preserve of young men from
wealthy upper-class families and from the aristocracy. They
brought their luxurious style to Oxford, attended by "scouts" or
servants in their rooms and spent ostentatiously and without concern. Intellectual brilliance was not required of them; theirs was a
social brilliance bestowed by class. There was another group at
Oxford, too, the "poor scholars." Tolkien, of course, was of this
group, and this was the group that predominated at his college,
Exeter. They were young men who had to be of exceptional merit.
Tolkien easily made friends with companions of this sort. At
Exeter, too, there was a group of Roman Catholic students who
helped ease his newness into familiarity.

During his first year at Oxford, Tolkien also stayed in touch
with old friends at King Edward. The other members of T.C.B.S.
were still there. Christmas of 1911, he returned to King Edward's
to perform the role of Mrs. Malaprop in a production of eighteenth century playwright, Richard Brinsley Sheridan's *The Rivals*
that his friend Rob Gilson was directing for the Christmas play.
They were still the same high-spirited boys they had always been.
Before the performance, they went out to a tea-shop in town in
their costumes. They wore their overcoats in the train, but took
them off in the shop causing stares and raised eyebrows. Some of
the boys, Tolkien, for one, were dressed as women.

Tolkien played rugby at Oxford. He joined the Essay Club and
the Dialectical Society and participated in Stapledon, the debating
society. He also started a club he called the Apolausticks, "those
who are devoted to self-indulgence." Its members read papers,

talked and argued together. They also held grand dinners in each other's rooms. Tolkien often found himself in debt when his weekly college expenses bill was presented. Having less money than he needed plagued Tolkien throughout most of his life (even when the cause no longer was extravagance). He couldn't afford a secretary to type the manuscript of *The Lord of the Rings* when he had to send it to his publisher, and he used typewriter ribbons until they were worn down. A don's salary was not enough to keep a wife and four children. Consequently, summers he took on extra work correcting State Certificate Exams for English secondary school pupils. Finally, the huge success of his books made him a multi-millionaire.

At Oxford, he was not only sometimes injudicious in the expenditure of money but could be absolutely rowdy in pursuing fun and in the practice of pranks. A great fan of The Marx Brothers' movies, throughout his life Tolkien was playful, liked pranks, costumes and incongruous comedy. "I have a very simple sense of humour," he wrote, "which even my appreciative critics find tiresome." Long after his high-spirited performances at King Edward's and the town-gown rowdiness of his Oxford days, when he was a don at Oxford, Tolkien was known to "dress up as An Anglo-Saxon warrior complete with axe and chase an astonished neighbour." He and C.S. Lewis once went to a party, which was not a costume party, as polar bears, Tolkien wearing a sheep skin and his face painted white." (Carpenter, *Tolkien*: 130) In the middle of an academic lecture, he might take a four inch green shoe from out of his pocket as proof that leprechauns exist, and in old age he might hand a store clerk his false teeth with the coins. (Birzer, 5)

Tolkien was "reading" Classics at Oxford, but there was no Classics tutor at Exeter College during his first year. His lax application to studies, however, was less a consequence of that than of the fact that he was bored with Greek and Roman authors. He kept working by himself on his own invented languages. And he was interested in the comparative philological study of the Germanic languages. Joseph Wright taught the classes and gave the lectures in Comparative Philology. This was the same Joseph

Wright who was the author of the Gothic textbook that had so excited Tolkien at King Edward's. Wright also introduced Tolkien to the study of Welsh, the language which had fascinated him when he saw it stenciled on coal cars in King's Heath Station when he lived as a boy in Birmingham. Explaining his love of Welsh, Token wrote:

> Most English-speaking people … will admit that cellar door is "beautiful", especially if dissociated from its sense (and its spelling) … Well then, in Welsh for me cellar doors are extraordinarily frequent.
>
> (Carpenter, *Tolkien:* 57)

Joseph Wright was also important to Tolkien because of his background. Like Tolkien's, Wright's was a story of adversity, individual striving, and prodigious accomplishment. The story of Wright's life recalls the plot of a novel by Charles Dickens. Employed in a woolen mill from the age of six, Wright was illiterate until he taught himself to read and write when he was fifteen because he envied the other workers around him their ability to read the newspapers. Once he'd accomplished that, he went to night school and learned French and German. In addition, he taught himself Latin and mathematics. At eighteen, he started a school in his bedroom in the cottage he shared with his widowed mother. At twenty-one, using the money he'd saved from this enterprise, he sailed to Antwerp and from there walked to Heidelberg and earned a doctorate in philology.

Tolkien had the same lively interest in language and learning that Wright had and a similar independent attitude. At Oxford he continued painting and drawing and was particularly fond of sketching landscapes. He practiced calligraphy and mastered a number of handwritings that he continued to use throughout his life. He continued to work on devising alphabets and inventing languages. He studied Finnish, which he loved and which influenced his own work both in the invention of languages and in the creation of literature. Finnish was the inspiration for "Quenya" or "High-elven," a language that appears in his stories. He wanted to read the *Kalevala* in Finnish, and he became proficient enough to do more than that. Of the value of the *Kalevala* itself, he wrote in a paper delivered to one of the literary societies at Oxford:

> These mythological ballads are full of that very primitive under-growth that the literature of Europe has on the whole been steadily cutting and reducing for many centuries with different and earlier completeness among different people. I would that we had more of it left—something of the same sort that belonged to the English.
>
> (Carpenter, *Tolkien:* 59)

Essentially replacing that lost mythology was his life work, and his books are the result. He wanted to make a mythology for the English. He invented tales using the English landscape, which he knew intimately. His hobbits are derivations from the English peasantry and middle-class, which, by his day, were often industrialized and landless. He admired the men from the lower classes when he saw their quiet endurance of trench war-fare and when he saw them respond to his subject during his years teaching at Leeds, where, unlike at Oxford, the students mainly came from the working class. In 1969, he wrote about teaching such students:

> A surprisingly large portion prove "educable": for which a primary qualification is the willingness to do some work…. (This willing-ness usually connotes some degree of humility. In Yorkshire [at Leeds] its first impulse was the desire to "get on." But this does not remain the sole objective.
>
> (Carpenter, ed., *Letters:* 403)

In 1912, he spent Christmas with his mother's sister May and her husband near Birmingham. He wrote a play they performed for the holiday. It was called "The Bloodhound, the Chef, and the Suffragette." A spoof on detective melodrama though it was, the entertainment nevertheless mirrored Tolkien's actual situation with regard to Edith. A world-famous Sherlock Holmes type detective is searching for a lost heiress…. She … has fallen in love with a penniless student whom she meets while they are living in the same lodging-house, and she has to remain undiscovered by her father until her twenty-first birthday in two days' time, after which she will be free to marry.

(Carpenter, *Tolkien:* 59)

The circumstances were like Tolkien's. On January 3, 1913, he turned twenty-one. That day he wrote to Edith, asking her to marry him. Her response was disquieting but not daunting. She wrote back telling him she was engaged to be married, but she also told him that it was not a marriage she was entering into for love, but because she felt "on the shelf." She wrote, "I began to doubt you Ronald and to think you would cease to care for me." (Carpenter, *Tolkien:* 61) On January 8, Tolkien took the train to Cheltenham and Edith met him at the station. After they walked in the countryside and talked about themselves, Edith accepted Tolkien's proposal and broke off with George Field, the young man she had agreed to marry, and gave him back his ring. Tolkien and Edith agreed not to announce their engagement or to marry until his schooling was completed and his future was more settled. But Tolkien did write to Father Francis, and was pleased when his benefactor did not oppose his wish.

At Oxford, Tolkien was going for a degree in Classics. To earn the degree, he had to pass two examinations. Upon his return from Cheltenham and recovering Edith he had to prepare for the first of these, called "Honour Moderations," a series of papers covering the candidate's field, in his case, Classics. Tolkien was brilliant, but he also could be an unconscientious student, devoted more to his private pursuits—inventing languages, drawing, staying up late with friends for conversation around the fire as they smoked their pipes—than to his studies. So Tolkien was relieved when he received a Second. But as a scholarship recipient, he was expected to do better. He ought to have passed with a First, especially because he intended to pursue an academic career. He knew as well as his teachers that he would have, had he applied himself. His paper on Comparative Philology, however, was what was called a pure alpha, a flawless paper. Because of this, and knowing Tolkien's interest in Old and Middle English and in Germanic languages in general, the Rector of Exeter, Dr. Lewis Farnell suggested that Tolkien change his field of specialization from Classics to English "avowedly as a pure philologue with no liking at all for English." (Carpenter, ed., *Letters*: 397)

The English section was itself split in two between "Language" and "Literature." The Language section dealt with literature up through Chaucer. The Literature section went from 1400 through the nineteenth century. Tolkien, of course, joined the Language division and specialized in linguistic studies. Kenneth Sisam, just four years his senior, became his tutor. At his invitation, Tolkien compiled the Middle-English dictionary published in 1922. In 1925 Sisam was also a candidate for the Oxford professorship to which Tolkien was appointed. Not as colorful a personality as Joseph Wright, Sisam was, however, a good scholar. Under his guidance Tolkien worked hard and wrote essays on "Problems of the dissemination of phonetic change," "The lengthening of vowels in Old and Middle English times," and "The Anglo-Norman element in English." (Carpenter, *Tolkien*: 64)

At the same time that Tolkien was pursuing Old English philological study he was also reading. He discovered the Icelandic Eddas: the Prose Edda, also called the Younger Edda and the Elder Edda. The Eddas collected oral lore in a body of mythological, heroic, folk tales written in prose and verse. And he continued reading Anglo-Saxon literature. He was especially excited by a group of Anglo-Saxon religious poems, called the *Crist*, by the eighth century Anglo-Saxon poet Cynewulf and others. Tolkien described his reaction to these lines from the *Crist*:

Eala Earendel engla beorhtast
Ofer middangeard monnum sended.
(Hail Earendel, brightest of angels
above the middle-earth sent unto men.)

saying that:

I felt a curious thrill as if something had stirred in me, half wakened from sleep. There was something very remote and strange and beautiful behind those words, if I could grasp it, far beyond ancient English.

(Carpenter, Tolkien: 64)

The degree to which these lines are important is clear if only because of the use of the term, middle-earth, which Tolkien made his own in *The Hobbit* and *The Lord of the Rings*. Additionally, however, they are important because of their influence on his imagination, beginning with the poem he wrote as a result of reading these verses. He was staying on his brother Hilary's farm at the end of the long, or summer, vacation in 1914 when he composed "The Voyage of Earendel the Evening Star."

The poem's conceit is that the star Earendel in the Anglo-Saxon poem had first been a sea vessel which moved from the ocean to the sky. In the early part of 1915, Tolkien took up the myth of Earendel again when he decided that he did not want to write separate and individual poems, but poems bound to each other by a common theme or through the development of a connecting narrative myth. He planned a series of poems, then, to be called "The Lay of Earendel." Later, Tolkien wove Earendel into the body of his mythology and into *The Hobbit* and *The Lord of the Rings* in several places. After Strider recites the love story of Beren and Luthien for Sam Gamgee in *The Lord of the Rings*, he tells of Earendel in order to explain the lineage of Elrond, the elf-lord, to whose land they are journeying. [I.ii.256] Tolkien makes Earendel the child of the species-crossed lovers, the mortal Beren and the immortal elf-maiden Lúthien of *The Silmarillion* and Earendel is the father of Elrond. (Carpenter, ed., *Letters:* 347) Tolkien had already begun, while he was in the trenches in France, to write poetry in one of his invented languages, and decided that it was Elven, a language spoken by Elves whom Earendel saw on his voyage. (Elven, later, is introduced into the linguistic fabric of *The Lord of the Rings*.) The first of these early poems, "The Shores of Faery," "tells of the mysterious land of Valinor, where two trees grow, one bearing golden sun-apples and the other silver moon-apples." (Carpenter, *Tolkien*: 76) (The light from those trees, when they are destroyed, is captured in the jewels called the Silmarils, from which: *The Silmarillion*.) Earendel passes through Valinor on Earth before his metamorphosis into a star. With "Earendel" Tolkien began to develop a mythology of his own and to integrate his "mad hobby" (Carpenter, ed., *Letters*: 8) of inventing languages into his poetry.

Tolkien altered the spelling to Earendil, when he made the tale the matter for Bilbo's song in Book II, Chapter I, "Many Meetings" of *The Fellowship of the Ring*, the first volume of *The Lord of the Rings*. He had composed the song during his years at Leeds. Randal Helms argues that there is also a parallel between Earendil's story and Frodo's in *The Lord of the Rings*:

> Earendil is given, quite without desiring it, a Silmaril; then after chaotic adventures, he passes to Elvenhome. A ship is built for him, and, all unwillingly, he leaves Middle-earth "to sail the shoreless skies" and "bear his shining lamp afar,/ the Flammifer of westernesse," becoming a star "till Moon should fade." This ... sounds much like Frodo's story: Quite without his willing it, Frodo is given the Ring, bears it through chaotic adventures, returns home, and then again, quite without willing or desiring it, must embark upon an elven-ship and pass westward, never to see again the simple haunts of hobbits.
>
> (Helms: 137)

At the time he wrote the first Earendel, Tolkien wrote other poems, too. Among them was "The Man in the Moon Came Down Too Soon,"—which became the song which brought Frodo to a fall when he performed an encore of it with too much mimetic merriment in I, ix, "At the Sign of the Prancing Pony," in *The Fellowship of the Ring*. His poem "Goblin Feet" was accepted by Blackwell's and published in the annual volume of *Oxford Poetry*. Reflecting Tolkien's abiding interests, the poems are rich with descriptions of fairies and countryside.

There was one other literary ingredient necessary for Tolkien to incorporate before he was ready to undertake his own epic invention. That was the work of William Morris. Morris was a complex, multi-talented figure of the nineteenth-century. He was a poet, writer of prose romances, translator, painter, designer, decorator, printer, furniture manufacturer, weaver, and utopian anarchist revolutionary. Like Tolkien, he had been an undergraduate at Exeter College, Oxford. Like Tolkien, too, Morris was distressed by the dehumanizing and nature-destroying technology of the industrial age, and he had a strong attraction to medievalism and to the Northern Sagas. He collaborated on a translation of the Icelandic *Volsungasaga.* He also wrote epics and romances like *The House of the Wolfings, The Earthly Paradise,* and *The Well at the World's End* in the manner of the ancient sagas he loved for their primitive aesthetic strength, their romantic ideals, and their freedom from the taint of industrial culture. Tolkien was drawn to Morris for his archaic language, his heroic plots, and for the painterly attention to detail with which Morris made his fantasy landscapes take on the dimensions of reality. He used Morris' epic saga imitations as models for his own early work. Tolkien's story of Kullervo, for example,—Kullervo commits incest unwittingly and throws himself on his sword when he discovers it—comes from the Finnish *Kalevala.* The *Kalevala* tale served as the basis for a romance in mixed prose and verse which Tolkien attempted to compose in the manner of Morris but never completed.

During his first year at Oxford, Tolkien had let his practice of Catholicism slip. But at the time of his engagement to Edith, he began to go to Mass and make Confession regularly, a practice he would sustain for the rest of his life, lapsing from time to time, but returning to the practice. He wrote to Michael in 1963,

> I fell in love with the Blessed Sacrament from the beginning—and by the mercy of God never have fallen out again: but alas! I indeed did not live up to it.... Out of wickedness and sloth I almost ceased to practice my religion—especially at Leeds, and at [Oxford, when living at] 22 Northmoor Road [during the years 1920–1929].
>
> (Carpenter, ed., *Letters:* 340)

Generally Tolkien went to early Mass daily and took his children, too. His oldest son, John became a Roman Catholic priest.

Edith was not a Roman Catholic. In order for Tolkien to take her as his wife, she had to become one. She did, not out of a love for the faith, but rather as a sign of her love for Ronald Tolkien. She studied with the parish priest, Father Murphy, and on January 8, 1914,—the anniversary of their reunion after the three years separation—she became a Roman Catholic. Soon afterwards, Father Murphy formally betrothed her and Tolkien in the Roman Catholic Church in Warwick. At first, Edith was apparently happy to take the Roman Catholic sacraments. At least Tolkien thought so. He wrote, for example, after they had attended Benediction that they "came away supremely happy, for it was the first time that we had ever been able to go calmly side by side to church." (Carpenter, *Tolkien*: 66) Perhaps it was so, or so it appeared to Tolkien. Edith's representation comes down to us almost completely through her husband, and biographers record nearly nothing of her but the little he presented. In any event, if Edith was delighted in the ceremonies of her new faith, it was not for long because, according to Humphrey Carpenter, "she began to dislike making her confession," and:

> she reported to Ronald that getting up to go to church early in the morning and fasting until she had made her communion did not agree with her. "I want to go," she told him, "and wish I could go often, but it is quite impossible: my health won't stand it."
>
> (Carpenter, *Tolkien:* 68-9)

Edith's ill health became a lifelong affliction.

Nearly from the time of their engagement, Edith lived in Tolkien's shadow. His life became hers. Humphrey Carpenter reports that during their period of engagement, while she was living in Warwick away from the familiar world she had known and been part of for three years in Cheltenham, "she was irritated to receive letters from Ronald describing a life at Oxford that was full of dinner parties, 'rags' [i.e., practical jokes], and visits to the cinematograph." (Carpenter, *Tolkien:* 69) Carpenter reports that at this time, too, while Edith really was "on the shelf," as she had earlier feared she was when she was waiting for Tolkien's twenty-first birthday, Tolkien was active socially and intellectually. He decorated his room with Japanese furniture and prints. He had two new suits tailor made. Every Saturday, he regularly took dinner in his friend Colin Cullis's rooms. He was elected president of the Exeter debating society. He played tennis and went boating. And he won the Skeat Prize for English in the Spring of 1914. With the prize money he bought several volumes of the works of William Morris.

Edith had not resisted becoming a Roman Catholic, but it was not something that she very much wanted either, and leaving the Church of England entailed a great deal of difficulty for her. She had told Tolkien that she wanted to wait to join the Roman Catholic faith until right before they were married. She anticipated the reaction against her, especially that she would be turned out of doors by her benefactor, and, indeed, she was when he found out, for Tolkien would not accept a delay in her conversion. Tolkien had not doubted Edith would suffer adverse responses to her conversion, but did not think that sufficient reason to wait. It was something his mother had had to endure, and if she could, it seemed to him, so, too, could Edith. Moreover, he disliked the Anglican Church. He called it "a pathetic and shadowy medley of half-remembered traditions and mutilated beliefs." (Carpenter, *Tolkien:* 65) He was deeply committed to Roman Catholicism, and believed, having seen his mother's determination and endurance, that faith may demand suffering: "I do so dearly believe," he wrote to Edith, "that no half-heartedness and no worldly fear must turn us aside from following the light unflinchingly." (Carpenter, *Tolkien:* 66) Looking back over their lives to come, however, it appears to have been more his light than hers.

Having to find a place to live was not the only concern for Edith. She belonged to the Church of England and had an active life and many friendships because of her involvement in its activities. She had to leave a place where she had established herself. She did not find the same social climate and personal fulfillment in Warwick or in the Roman Catholic Church that she had in Cheltenham and in the Church of England. Moreover, as her frequent absence from church-going indicates, the strictness of Roman Catholic religious discipline did not appeal to her as it did to Tolkien.

In 1914, the madness of the First World War was becoming all consuming. When Tolkien returned to Oxford in the fall of that year, it was a different place. "It is awful," he wrote, "I really don't think I shall be able to go on: work seems impossible. Not a single man I know is up except Cullis." (Carpenter, *Tolkien*: 72) Geoffrey Smith, the poet and one of the members of the T.C.B.S. at King Edward, he later discovered, was also still there. But nearly everyone else had signed up for the war, including his brother Hilary, who served as a bugler. There had been pressure from his family for him to enlist also. But he was determined to earn his degree first. In a letter to Michael, in 1941, towards the beginning of the Second World War, Tolkien described his situation at the start of the First:

> … war broke out… I still had a year to go at college. In those days, chaps joined up, or were scorned publicly. It was a nasty cleft to be in, especially for a young man with too much imagination and little physical courage. No degree: no money: no fiancée. I endured the obloquy, and hints becoming outspoken from relatives, stayed up [at Oxford], and produced a First in Finals in 1915. Bolted into the Army; July 1915. I found the situation intolerable and married on March 22, 1916. May found me crossing the Channel (I still have the verse I wrote on the occasion!) for the carnage of the Somme.
>
> (Carpenter, ed., *Letters:* 53)

While still at Oxford, Tolkien enrolled in a program that allowed him to do army training but to defer the actual call-up until after getting his degree. (Carpenter, *Tolkien*: 72) He combined study with army drill, and he lived in rooms of his own, "digs," which he shared with Colin Cullis, who had not enlisted because of ill-health. About the training he wrote to Edith in November 1915, "The usual kind of morning standing about and freezing and then trotting to get warmer so as to freeze again. We ended up by an hour's bomb-throwing with dummies." (Carpenter, ed., *Letters*: 8)

Christmas vacation that year, Tolkien went to London for a reunion of the T.C.B.S. at Christopher Wiseman's house. They, of course, did not know that it was the last time the four of them would ever meet like that, sitting around a gas fire, smoking their pipes, and talking in a way that, Tolkien wrote, helped him develop "a voice for all kinds of pent up things." But given the climate of the world and their imminent rendezvous with death, there must have been an intensity to their gathering. He referred to their reunion as The Council of London. Soon after, Tolkien began his "Lay of Earendel". (Carpenter, ed., *Letters*: 10)

In June 1915, Tolkien passed his Oxford graduation examinations with a First, guaranteeing him an academic career once the war was over. But for him the war was just beginning. His commission was as a second lieutenant in the Lancashire Fusiliers, thirteenth battalion. They began training in July 1915 at Bedford. He was lodged in the town in a house with six other officers, of whom he wrote: "Gentlemen are non-existent among the superiors, and even human beings are rare indeed." (Carpenter, *Tolkien*: 78) About the entire enterprise he wrote: "These grey days wasted in wearily going over, over and over again, the dreary topics, the dull backwaters of the art of killing, are not enjoyable." All the same, in character with his way of following the world outwardly while inwardly following either the course of his religion or fantasy invention, Tolkien performed what he took to be his duty. He studied Morse code and how to do flag, disc heliograph, and lamp signaling. He learned how to operate field telephones and fire signal rockets and how to handle carrier pigeons. (Carpenter, *Tolkien*: 78)

Tolkien's experience in the war, until it became horrible beyond endurance was disquieting from the first. From Calais on June 6, the day of arrival, Tolkien's battalion was sent to their base camp at Etaples. During this part of his trip, his entire kit was lost: his camp bed, sleeping bag, mattress, spare boots, and washstand. There were no replacements to be reissued because these things had not been issued in the first place. It was each soldier's responsibility to supply himself with these things or go without. Now, Tolkien had to get supplies as he could. As during training in England, Tolkien disliked many of the men he was forced to be with: he complained about the narrowness of his superiors, and their unkindness, that "they treated him like an inferior schoolboy." (Carpenter, *Tolkien*: 81) This was largely the result of the ranking system at the core of military organization. When his battalion moved from Etaples to the front, marching through the Picardy country side of poppy and mustard fields, on dusty roads or, under torrents of rain, through muddy ones, and then billeted in the hamlet of Rubempré, the officers slept in camp beds in the farmhouses. The common soldiers slept on straw in the barns. In general, fraternization between the officers and the "men" was not permitted. Tolkien got to know several of the common soldiers, and to admire them, only through the contact he had with those who served as "batmen" to him, that is as his servants. Many years later, after the publication of *The Lord of the Rings*, Tolkien wrote that the character Sam Gamgee, the loyal and heroic hobbit who goes along with Frodo on his quest "is a reflexion of the English soldier, of the privates and batmen I knew in the 1914 war, and recognised as so far superior to myself." (Carpenter, *Tolkien*: 81)

CHAPTER FOUR

At Leeds and Oxford

It [Fantasy] certainly does not destroy or even insult Reason; and it does not either blunt the appetite for, nor obscure the perception of, scientific veracity. On the contrary. The keener and the clearer is the reason, the better fantasy will it make....

—Tolkien (*Tree and Leaf,* 54)

IF A LIFE CAN BE DIVIDED into phases, Tolkien's would fit—despite his dislike for Shakespeare—quite neatly into seven ages: his first years in Bloemfontein up through the death of his father; his childhood in Sarehole with his mother until her death; his school years at King Edward and then Oxford; his experience of the First World War; his entering into his professional career at Leeds; his long tenure at Oxford; and his success as the author of *The Hobbit* and *The Lord of the Rings.*

For Tolkien, the First World War effectively ended his youth— "I bemoaned the collapse of all my world that began just after I achieved 21," he wrote to Michael in 1968 (Carpenter, ed., *Letters:* 393)—and darkened his vision of things. The deaths of millions of young men intruded as a reality into his life and into the lives of most of the men of his generation. Death's presence, and the absurd and brutal voracity of war, forced upon him the

closing question so desperately put by his friend Geoffrey Smith.
It was in a letter written some five months before Smith himself
was killed by a shell blast and the gangrenous effects of exposure
to poison gas:

> 15 July 1916.
>
> My dear John Ronald,
>
> I saw in the paper this morning that Rob [Gilson, one of the
> four King Edward friends who made up the T.C.B.S.] has been
> killed.
>
> I am safe but what does that matter?
>
> Do please stick to me, you and Christopher [Wiseman, another
> of the four]. I am very tired and most frightfully depressed at this
> worst of news.
>
> Now one realises in despair what the T.C.B.S. really was.
>
> O my dear John Ronald what ever are we going to do?
>
> Yours ever,
G.B.S.
(Carpenter, Tolkien: 84)

The T.C.B.S. had offered a vision of a world entirely different
from the hell the war cast them into. The T.C.B.S. was a fellowship founded on creativity and hope, not a comradeship forged
from shared despair wrought by destruction both incalculable and
incomprehensible.

It is not difficult to see the remainder of Tolkien's long life as a
practical meditation on G.B.S.'s plaintive question, "what ever are
we going to do?" In his work, Tolkien is asserting the meaning of
creation they believed in during their youth in the face of the great
challenge that the First World War posed against it, even by using
that challenge as his work's theme. The world had failed him; it
had become absurd, and not only for him, but from his philosophical standpoint, for all of mankind. Certainly, his strong
adherence to the Roman Catholic faith gave Tolkien the perspective that he lived in a fallen world, which ultimately was unreliable
and could not be depended upon, and that there was a blessed and
eternal world around it, which was absolutely sure and had not

become absurd. But that was not his only response. He did not find comfort in passivity, resignation or asceticism. He set out to make as much as he could of the fallen world. It became Tolkien's life work to propose and to realize through literature another world without challenging and subverting the one of his religious faith. He dedicated himself to creating a complex organic fantasy or mythic world, which nevertheless encompassed the evil power of negation and destruction.

The two forces that Tolkien would harness in this endeavor were learning and creativity. Both involve the processes of life and the ways of the human spirit. Through learning the intellect analyzes the world, discovering its components, and by the act of creation those components are reformed and reassembled in the construction of a world more accessible. Tolkien came to prefer to call the act of human creativity sub-creation rather than creation. For him it was creation inside the Creation. It was the act through which "man" most was like God, but, because it was an act of fantasy but not delusion, it was free from the taint of *hybris*. "Fantasy is a natural human activity," he wrote:

> (…) If men were ever in a state in which they did not want to know or could not perceive truth (facts or evidence), then Fantasy would languish until they were cured. If they ever get into that state … Fantasy will perish, and become Morbid Delusion.
>
> (*Tree and Leaf:* 54)

After the war he returned to the work, which he had embarked upon before the war, of creating a mythology that would serve as a foundation for a great work of literature. The war made such work that much more meaningful and necessary.

At the armistice, Tolkien put in a request, which was granted, that, until his demobilization, he be posted in Oxford "for the purpose of completing [his] education." (Carpenter, *Tolkien:* 98) He had been invited to work as a philologist on *The New English Dictionary*, popularly known as the O.E.D., the *Oxford English Dictionary*. The dictionary was begun in 1878. In 1900 the first part comprising entries from A to H was published. Eighteen years later, partly because of the war and partly because of the death of its original editor, Sir James Murray, in 1915, the second half was not yet ready. Entries falling under the letters U to Z still were left. Tolkien had the words *warm, wasp, water, wick (lamp),* and *winter* to define. Dr. Henry Bradley, after Murray's death, the supervisor of the project, wrote of him:

> His work gives evidence of an unusually thorough mastery of Anglo-Saxon and the facts and principles of the comparative grammar of the Germanic languages. Indeed, I have no hesitation in saying that I have never known a man of his age who was in these respects his equal.
>
> (4: 101)

Tolkien later remarked, "I learned more in those two years than in any other equal period of my life." (Carpenter, *Tolkien:* 101)

He did not work full days at the office of the Dictionary, however. He also saw pupils from Oxford sent to him by its several colleges. Because he was married, he was able to see female students in his home—his wife was there—without their needing to bring a chaperone along. He began making enough money for him to move Edith and the baby to better rooms in Oxford.

In 1920, Tolkien applied for the post of Reader in English Language at the University of Leeds, although he did not expect to get it. He was interviewed by, and thus made the acquaintance of, George Gordon, then Professor of English at Leeds. Five years later when Tolkien applied for the professorship of Anglo-Saxon at Oxford, George Gordon, who had moved there from Leeds in 1922, swung the vote in his favor.

From the very beginning of his years at Leeds, Tolkien seems to have considered Leeds as a step on the way rather than a place to stop. After the first year he responded to two invitations to be a candidate for professorships of the English Language, one in Liverpool and one in Cape Town, South Africa. He was not chosen at Liverpool, but he was offered the job in South Africa. Knowing it would put an impossible strain on Edith and the baby, he decided not to move his family. But the prospect was alluring. He had been born in South Africa, and his father had died there, buried in a grave his son had never seen.

Early in 1922, E.V. Gordon became a junior lecturer at Leeds. Gordon was a Canadian who had come to Oxford on a Rhodes scholarship, and in 1920, Tolkien had been his tutor. They became good friends and collaborators. Tolkien wrote in his diary, "Eric Valentine Gordon has come and got firmly established and is my devoted pal." (Carpenter, *Tolkien:* 104)

At the time of Gordon's arrival Tolkien was compiling a glossary, really a small dictionary, for a book of Medieval extracts edited by Kenneth Sisam. Sisam, only four years his senior, had been Tolkien's tutor at Oxford, and was the man Tolkien would beat out for the Professorship of Anglo-Saxon at Oxford in 1925. In 1971, Tolkien wrote, remembering Sisam:

> His teaching was ... spiced with a pungency, humor and practical wisdom which were his own. I owe him a great debt and have not forgotten it.... [T]he foundation of my library was laid by Sisam. He taught me not only to read texts, but to study second-hand book catalogues.
>
> (Carpenter, ed., *Letters:* 406)

The glossary was published in 1922. Tolkien was then available to work on a project with E.V. Gordon. They decided to compile a new edition of the Middle English poem, *Sir Gawain and the Green Knight.* Tolkien edited the text and compiled the glossary. Gordon annotated the text. It was published in 1925 and came to be regarded as a major work of scholarship and remains the standard text.

Edith, in 1920, was not glad to move to Leeds. But once there, despite the fact that Leeds lacked the beauty or the grandeur of Oxford she liked living there. The very lack of the formality and intellectual snobbery—as she felt it—which she sensed in Oxford suited her, and she made friends with many of the other faculty wives. In October, she gave birth to Michael, their second child. Tolkien, too, despite his cramped office facilities and the general ugliness of the surroundings, liked it. His philological work went well. Students and faculty liked him. He discovered that he was good at teaching. He was convivial, too, and, with E. V. Gordon, he founded the Viking Club for undergraduates. The members met to drink beer, read sagas aloud and sing comic songs in Anglo-Saxon and Old Norse, which often had been written by Tolkien and Gordon. Years later some of the verses were printed as *Songs for Philologists*, and one of them appeared in the 1950s in the musical review by Flanders and Swann, *At the Drop of A Hat.*

Tolkien's popularity drew more students than ever to specialize in linguistics. He described that accomplishment and his way of teaching in the letter of application he sent to the Electors for the Rawlinson and Bosworth Professorship of Anglo-Saxon at Oxford in June, 1925. At Leeds, he wrote, he was given "a free commission to develop the linguistic side of a large and growing School of English Studies, in which no regular provision had as yet been made for the linguistic specialist." (Carpenter, ed., *Letters*: 12–13)

In the midst of his university activities, Tolkien kept working at his own writing. Some of his verse was printed in the Leeds University magazine, *The Gryphon*, some in a local magazine, *Yorkshire Poetry*, and some appeared in *Northern Ventures*, an anthology of poetry by members of the Leeds English Department. He also began a series of poems he called "Tales and Songs of Bimble Bay," which present themes and images which reappear in his major works. One tale is a protest against the mechanical character of modern life in cities, which, he decried to the end of his days. He also deplored the noise of the mechanized industrial world. In July 1964 he wrote to a friend how living in Oxford:

> became hellish as soon as petrol restrictions ceased [after the Second World War]. But Headington [the suburb of Oxford where he was then living] is no paradise of peace ... While the actual inhabitants do all that radio, tele, dogs, scooters, buzzbikes, and cars of all sizes but the smallest can do to produce noise from early morn to about 2 a.m.
>
> (Carpenter, ed., *Letters:* 345)

Another of the Bimble Bay tales introduced a dragon which

threatens Bimble Bay. Another described a cave-dwelling slimy creature with pale and luminous eyes, a precursor to Gollum, a character in the *Rings* trilogy. Tolkien also continued to work on parts of *The Silmarillion*. He was turning the prose version of his story about the lovers Beren and Lúthien into verse, calling the poem "The Gest of Beren and Lúthien." Later Tolkien renamed it "The Lay of Leithian" and used it as the basis for a story in *The Silmarillion*. "Of Beren and Lúthien," Chapter 19, like all the stories in *The Silmarillion* is written in prose, but at the beginning of the tale, the narrator explains that it is a prose retelling of a poem:

> Of their lives was made the Lay of Leithien, Release from Bondage, which is the longest save one of the songs concerning the world of old; but here the tale is told in fewer words and without song.

This layering and texturing is characteristic of Tolkien's work. It gives his fiction historical depth and narrative weight. The sense is conveyed that the tale we are reading is just one account of something that happened independently of this particular telling, and since it is derived from other narratives, a culture in which it has significant existence is suggested. It seems to exist independent of its author. It can appear, then, in diverse works as a piece of mythological lore—just as the Greek stories do. The tale of Beren and Lúthien is, in fact, incorporated into *The Lord of the Rings* at I, 204 when Strider sings their story to his companions. Elrond, the elf-lord at whose house Frodo meets Bilbo and Gandalf again in II. i. is their descendent. Tolkien, rather than being the author of the tale of Beren and Lúthien is cast as its recorder, a term he often used to refer to himself as a writer.

In 1923, Tolkien came down with a bad case of pneumonia. After he recovered, Tolkien, Edith and the two boys visited Tolkien's younger brother Hilary in Evesham, where, after the war he had bought a small orchard and a market garden. He had become a fruit farmer. He remained one all his life. They helped on the land with the farm work and enjoyed flying kites. Towards the end of their tenure at Leeds, in 1924, Edith became pregnant again, and Christopher was born in November of that year. In

1925, after he had been appointed Professor of Anglo-Saxon, Tolkien moved Edith and the three children back to Oxford. Although they changed houses several times, they did not leave the town until late in their lives, in 1968, after all the children—a fourth, Priscilla was born in 1929—had left home. Throughout his years in Oxford, Tolkien lived, to all appearances, the typical life of an Oxford don. "Unpretentious," Tolkien scholars and biographers Deborah Webster Rogers and Ivor A. Rogers called it, "like the wardrobe in C.S. Lewis's *The Lion, the Witch and the Wardrobe,* larger inside than outside." (Rogers, D. and I. Rogers: 27)

When Tolkien left Leeds University in 1925 to assume the Bosworth and Rawlinson Professorship at Oxford he had formulated all the interests and begun work on all the projects which were to engage him for the rest of his life. What lay ahead of him was constructing the edifice he had already imagined. For him to do that, his life at Oxford was particularly well-suited. It provided him with an established routine. Inside that routine he could devote himself to philology and literature. Equally committed to both these disciplines, Tolkien had one subject which manifested itself in two forms. Each, moreover, participated in the other. His study of language, as his lecture on *Beowulf* showed, was in the service of literature. His passion for storytelling grew from a love of language and from a desire to discover the worlds in which his constructed languages belonged and the nature of the creatures who spoke those languages and lived in those worlds. He himself then was a person seemingly with two lives or, at least, two careers, philologist and storyteller, but each nourished the other and together formed a unity.

Tolkien returned to Oxford in 1925, and at the beginning of 1926, he bought a modest house in Northmoor Road. Three years later he sold it and bought the house next door, a larger and grander looking ivy-covered place, with a slate roof and leaded windows. It had been owned by the bookseller, Basil Blackwell. It was the Tolkien family home for the next eighteen years.

Tolkien had to face division in the English School at Oxford, too. The rivalry was between the two fields that in him coexisted and also nurtured each other. At Oxford, the linguists resented literary intrusion and those interested in literature resented philological requirements. Tolkien lobbied for a change that would release literature students from having to take philology courses and that would no longer require language students to study post-Chaucerian literature. In addition, he sought to make the study of philology a study of literature alive to the reader, not a learned and detached examination of curious artifacts. Perhaps nowhere in Tolkien's writing is this idea more strongly and fancifully expressed than in an analogy presented in a lecture, *Beowulf: The Monsters and the Critics*, which he delivered to the British Academy in London on November 25, 1936.

Tolkien succeeded in convincing the English School faculty, in 1931, after a period of strong resistance, to institute his proposals. (Carpenter, *Tolkien:* 137)

In many ways, Tolkien fit the stereotype of what a don at Oxford should be like. Certainly, he looked the part. Desmond Albrow wrote in the *Catholic Herald* of seeing Tolkien at Oxford:

> He was a professor who looked like a professor.... Tolkien wore cords and a sports jacket, smoked a reassuring pipe, laughed a lot, sometimes mumbled when his thoughts outstripped words, looked in those days to my idealistic eyes like the young Leslie Howard, the film actor. There was a sense of civilization, winsome sanity and sophistication about him.
>
> (Tolkien, *P. and J. Tolkien:* 117)

Student response to Tolkien varied. T. V. Benn, one of Tolkien's students who later became a teacher at Leeds, reported that "Tolkien was liked as a lecturer. He was not eloquent but quiet and factual and friendly." (Grotta-Kurska: 63) Certainly his quick and mumbling speech got in the way. Geoffrey Woledge, a student of Tolkien's who also became a teacher at Leeds, recalled Tolkien's way of teaching:

> It was mostly a line-by-line commentary—sometimes barely audible. It was generally found very wearisome; I generally sat in the back, talked in whispers to my neighbors, or wrote poetry or letters.

Nevertheless, in after years I have come to think that the most valuable thing I owe to my university teachers was his teaching, not indeed of the texts he was lecturing on, but of the way in which antiquarian scholarship can be used to illuminate literature.

(Grotta-Kurska: 62)

Woledge also recalled what happened when they cut one of Tolkien's classes.

Once, he had not arrived at the lecture room five minutes after the lecture should have started, and I and two friends decided to spend an hour in a neighboring pub; as we were nearing the end of the corridor leading from the lecture room, he suddenly appeared around the corner. We stopped in some confusion, but he waved his class register cheerily, said, "Shall I mark you absent?" And passed on, leaving us to pursue our quest for refreshment.

(Grotta-Kurska: 63)

Another former pupil, J.I.M. Stewart, who later wrote detective stories under the name Michael Innes (Rogers, D. and I. Rogers: 25), responded differently to Tolkien's classroom manner: "He could turn a lecture room into a mead hall in which he was the bard and we were the feasting, listening guests." W. H. Auden also had been a student of his, and years later, when they were friends wrote him, "I don't think I have ever told you what an unforgettable experience it was for me as an undergraduate, hearing you recite *Beowulf*. The voice was the voice of Gandalf." (Carpenter, *Tolkien:* 133) What nearly all his students seem to agree on about Tolkien, despite his mumbling and wandering, was that he was a "deeply sympathetic man," and a kind man who "treated nearly everyone well." (Birzer, 5) Perhaps the best way to get a sense of Tolkien as a teacher is to consider a contrast between him and C. S. Lewis made by Anthony Curtis, who had been a student of both.

At the end of the hour with Lewis I always felt a complete ignoramus; no doubt an accurate impression but also a rather painful one; and if you did venture to challenge one of his theories the ground was cut away from beneath your feet with lightning speed. It was a fool's mate in three moves with Lewis smiling at you from the other side of the board in unmalicious glee at his victory. By contrast Tolkien was the soul of affability. He did all the talking, but he made you feel you were his intellectual equal. Yet his views beneath the deep paternal charm were passionately held.

(Birzer, 4)

Tolkien enjoyed great popularity with students as well as their esteem, and his classes were full, often crowded by additional students who, although not registered for the class came to hear his lecture. He devoted himself to his teaching. Oxford statutes required that teachers like Tolkien give a minimum of thirty-six lectures or classes each year. In his second year at Oxford, Tolkien gave 136, taking upon himself so great a burden because the faculty was understaffed. Tolkien finally succeeded in opening a place for the appointment of a second philologist in the school, the Anglo-Saxon scholar Charles Wrenn, who was also a friend of Tolkien's and whose wife Agnes was one of Edith's few friends at Oxford. The two families even vacationed together in 1932 in Cornwall, where "Wrenn and Tolkien held a swimming race wearing panama hats and smoking pipes while they swam." (Carpenter, *Tolkien*: 160)

At Oxford, Tolkien was also expected as part of his professional duties to continue to do the sort of scholarly research and publication he had begun at Leeds. By 1925, he had already published the Middle English glossary, an edition of *Sir Gawain and the Green Knight,* which he had worked on in collaboration with E.V. Gordon, and chapters in *The Year's Work in English Studies* for 1923 and again for 1924 on "Philology, General Works," reviewing on-going work in the field. In 1925, he published "Some Contributions to Middle-English Lexicography," a short essay in the *Review of English Studies.* In 1929, Tolkien published an article on the *Ancrene Wisse. The Ancrene Wisse* is "a medieval book of instruction for a group of anchorites," [religious hermits]. (Carpenter, *Tolkien*: 134) It was written in the West

Midlands dialect that Tolkien was expert in and which he felt himself rooted in not just by scholarship. "I am," he wrote in a letter to W.H. Auden in 1955, "a West-midlander by blood (and took to early west-midland Middle English as a known tongue as soon as I set eyes on it)." (Carpenter, ed., *Letters*: 213) In a study of two original manuscripts of that text, one at Cambridge and one in the Bodleian Library at Oxford, Tolkien refuted assertions that the language of the *Ancrene Wisse* was primitive and lacking literary merit. He showed that the text was actually quite sophisticated literature.

When he returned to Oxford Tolkien began working on a scholarly edition of the Cambridge manuscript of the *Ancrene Wisse* and on an edition of an Anglo-Saxon poem called *Exodus*. These scholarly activities were overshadowed by his literary activity. Nevertheless, in the 1930s, Tolkien produced two outstanding pieces of work in his field. One was *Beowulf: the Monsters and the Critics*. The other was a paper on the regional English dialects which appear in Chaucer's *The Reeve's Tale* in *The Canterbury Tales*. It was delivered at a meeting of The Philological Society in 1931 and published in 1934. With his old collaborator, E.V. Gordon, he planned to put out editions of the great Middle English poem *Pearl*, thought to be by the same poet who wrote *Sir Gawain and the Green Knight*, and of the Anglo-Saxon Elegies *The Wanderer* and *The Seafarer*.

When Tolkien left Leeds, Gordon had been appointed to his place, but soon after, Gordon moved to the University of Manchester. He died at the age of forty-two from kidney failure in 1938. (Carpenter, *Tolkien*: 140) After Gordon's death, Tolkien planned to collaborate with Simonne d'Ardenne, a Belgian philologist who had studied Middle English with him and earned her degree from Oxford. They were going to do an edition of a Western Middle English text called *Katerine*. He had contributed significantly to d'Ardenne's edition of *The Life and Passion of St. Juliene*, like *Ancrene Wisse* and *Katerine*, a work in Western Middle English. The Second World War made that collaboration impossible. They did collaborate after the war on several short articles about the text of *Katerine*, but by then *The Lord of the Rings* had a hold on his attention.

Translation is another form of scholarship, especially when it is translation from an Anglo-Saxon or Middle English text. The original is, of course, not a printed thing but a manuscript or a number of manuscripts, which, as part of the work of translation, must be deciphered, collated, and interpreted. Some words may be unique, and their meaning or meanings must be discovered through philological and contextual evaluations and assumptions. Other words may suggest a variety of meanings from which the translator must choose. Therefore, while a translator does not offer a text of the original, the scholarship involved in making a translation is considerable and is, in fact, an elucidation or interpretation of an assumed original text. The translator, after all, must establish a text, even if only for him- or herself, from which to make the translation. Tolkien made translations of a number of important Middle English poems including *Sir Gawain, Pearl,* and *Sir Orfeo.* His translation of *Pearl* was finished in 1926 but Tolkien did not offer it for publication then.

Blackwell's was a bookshop in Oxford that Tolkien frequented, and he bought books on credit there. Blackwell's not only sold books. It also published them. In the 1940s, the firm offered to publish Tolkien's translation of *The Pearl.* His payment would be credited to his account, thus toward clearing his debt at the bookseller's. The publishers wanted him to write an introduction, but he was lax, and the book, set in type, was not printed. It is not known exactly when he did his translation of *Sir Gawain and the Green Knight,* but it was broadcast on BBC radio in 1953. For that broadcast, Tolkien did record an introduction and a talk about the work. After Tolkien became a renowned author with *The Hobbit* and *The Lord of the Ring,* his publisher, Allen & Unwin wanted to put out a volume containing both translations, *Pearl* and *Sir Gawain and the Green Knight.* Tolkien made extensive revisions in the texts, but seems to have been stymied again by the introduction, and the book was not published. It was only after his death that both translations along with his translation of another medieval poem, *Sir*

Orfeo were published. For this edition the introduction was done by Tolkien's younger son Christopher, who edited, collated, sometimes completed, and published the work his father left unfinished.

CHAPTER FIVE

Family

*In 1955, in response to the question, What makes
you tick? from Harvey Breit of The New York Times
Book Review, Tolkien replied, "I don't tick. I am not
a machine. (If I did tick, I should have no views on
it, and you had better ask the winder.)"*

(Birzer, 110)

TOLKIEN THE WRITER, Tolkien the teacher, Tolkien the scholar: all
were principal and complementary aspects of the same person, and
they are all public aspects. As such they are available to public
scrutiny. But there is another side to Tolkien which is more difficult to discover, essentially because Tolkien himself did not discuss
it publicly. That is his "private" life, his family life. To be discreet
about private things was the result of his disposition. It is also, rec-
ognizably, a significant characteristic of his culture. During his
three years of waiting for Edith, his friends knew nothing of their
story or of her existence. Tolkien and his friends talked about their
interests and their work, not about "themselves." When he
announced to the other members of the T.C.B.S. that he was
going to marry Edith, everything was a surprise to them. Similarly,
years later, Tolkien was surprised to learn, from a notice in *The
Times,* that C.S. Lewis, his closest friend, had gotten married.

Tolkien was a private person, despite his success in the academic world and then as a world-renown author of books, which have sold between one hundred and one hundred and fifty million copies. He did not seek or take to the spotlight, but he was well-known for responding to serious correspondence from readers who wrote him about his work. Certainly, he had no impulse to self-revelation or to sharing the details of his life. He thought knowledge of his biography had no bearing on a reader's enjoyment or understanding of his work. In a letter dated October 25, 1958, in response to a scholar who had written to him "because I was going to give a talk on him and there was little material in print," Tolkien wrote:

> I do not like giving "facts" about myself other than "dry" ones (which anyway are quite as relevant to my books as any other more juicy details). Not simply for personal reasons; but also because I object to the contemporary trend in criticism, with its excessive interest in the details of the lives of authors and artists. They only distract attention from an author's works ... and end ... in becoming the main interest.
>
> (Rogers, D. and I. Rogers: 125)

In a letter dated February 23, 1966, which Tolkien himself later called "a little tart," Tolkien wrote to the poet, and his friend, W.H. Auden, after Auden had informed him that he had contracted to write a book on Tolkien for a series called *Christian Perspectives:*

> I regret very much to hear that you have contracted to write a book about me. It does meet with my strong disapproval. I regard such things as premature impertinences: and unless undertaken by an intimate friend, or with consultation of the subject (for which I have at present no time), I cannot believe that they have a usefulness to justify the distaste and irritation given to the victim.
>
> (Carpenter, ed., *Letters:* 367)

And a few months later, in April, Tolkien wrote again to Auden regarding remarks Auden was reported by The New Yorker magazine and the London Daily Telegraph to have made before the New York Tolkien Society regarding Tolkien's house. Auden apparently said that Tolkien "lives in a hideous house—I can't tell you how awful it is—with hideous pictures on the walls." Tolkien let Auden know that "[t]his was the main item in reports in English papers and exposed my wife and myself to a certain amount of ridicule." (Carpenter, ed., Letters: 367–8)

A year later, February 8, 1967, Tolkien wrote to Charlotte and Denis Plimmer who had interviewed him for a feature in *The Daily Telegraph Magazine* and now wanted some pictures of him:

> In one point I fear that I shall disappoint you. I am informed that the Weekend Telegraph wishes to have your article illustrated by a series of pictures taken of me at work and at home. In no circumstances will I agree to being photographed again for such a purpose. I regard all such intrusions into my privacy as an impertinence, and I can no longer afford the time for it. The irritation it causes me spreads its influence over a far greater time than the actual intrusion occupies.
>
> (Carpenter, ed., *Letters:* 372)

An attempt to render an account of the relationship between Edith and Ronald Tolkien is fraught with peril for several reasons. Not the least of them is the awareness that both parties would consider it an intrusion and probably an exercise in gossip. Moreover there is very little detailed information a biographer has to go on. When Daniel Grotta-Kurska sought information from Michael Tolkien, Ronald and Edith's second son, for his unauthorized biography, Michael advised him that "it is my policy to keep all discussion about my father himself as far as possible strictly within the family, or those so long associated with it as to be virtually part of it." (Grotta-Kurska: 160) Humphrey Carpenter, authorized by Tolkien's heirs, after his death, to write his biography presents a broad outline of Edith's and Ronald's life together rather than details:

> [Tolkien] and Edith were still very different people with widely dif-
> ferent interests, and even after fifty years of marriage they were not
> always ideal company for each other. Occasionally there were
> moments of irritation between them, just as there had been
> throughout their lives. But there was still, as there always had been,
> great love and affection, perhaps even more now that the strain of
> bringing up a family had passed.
>
> (Carpenter, Tolkien: 245)

In 1981, a few years after his biography appeared, Carpenter in collaboration with Christopher Tolkien, edited a collection of Tolkien's letters. Carpenter reports that "an immense number of letters by Tolkien survive," and that he has had to choose but a few and that "[a]mong the omissions is the very large body of letters [Tolkien] wrote between 1913 and 1918 to Edith Bratt ... these are highly personal in character, and from them I have chosen only a few passages which refer to the writings in which Tolkien was engaged at the time." (Carpenter, ed., *Letters:* 1)

Tolkien's marriage to Edith lasted fifty-five years, until her death two years before his. Both the strengths and the weaknesses of their relationship, things which bound them together and things which divided them, are apparent from the earliest days of their association. They were both orphans, feeling the absence of family, and they formed a friendship, it can be assumed, based at least in part on their mutual need and common experience. They were also both high-spirited. They enjoyed the pilfered food they'd gotten from their parsimonious landlady's kitchen. They snuck off on their bicycles to drink tea in tea-shops. Father Francis Morgan's opposition to their romance strengthened it, transformed their young love into an authentic attachment, full of clandestine meetings, turmoil, and subsequent separation. "Nothing else" beside this opposition, Tolkien wrote to Michael in 1941, "would have hardened the will enough to give such an affair (however genuine a case of true love) permanence." (Carpenter, ed., *Letters:* 53)

Edith became an ideal and a goal for Ronald as well as the flesh and blood companion she had been. What Ronald was for Edith during the period of their three years' absolute separation is difficult to know. But while he did not surrender the hope of reuniting with her, she did not wait for him. When he wrote to her on the eve of his twenty-first birthday, she wrote back to tell him she was engaged. The obstacle did not deter but, rather, stimulated him. And he won her back. His resolute demand that she become Roman Catholic, despite her lack of any real calling to enter the Church, also shows how much their relationship was defined by him rather than by her. While this male-oriented determination was perfectly common and even apparently within the nature of things in 1916, it nevertheless, contributed to difficulties in the relationship. It is speculative, but reasonable to think it was at the root of domestic tension and irritation they both experienced and the resentment, social discomfort, and even chronic health complaints that Edith suffered.

In the first years of their marriage, Edith was a muse for Tolkien. She read his work and helped copy his early manuscripts. They took lovers' walks in a small wood in Roos in Yorkshire, and she danced in the woods for him. Tolkien described her: "Her hair was raven, her skin clear, her eyes bright, and she could sing—and dance." (Carpenter, *Tolkien*: 97) She became the model for Lúthien, the immortal Elf-Queen in "The Lay of Lúthien," who falls in love with the mortal Beren. Tolkien always identified himself and Edith with the lovers. Perhaps as much as a romantic idealization of their love, Tolkien's identification of Edith with Lúthien was a recognition of her as a woman, like Lúthien, who sacrificed herself to be united with her lover. So strong was the identification for Tolkien that those names are inscribed along with Ronald's and Edith's actual names on their tombstones. The story of Lúthien and Beren, which he rewrote in prose for *The Silmarillion,* additionally, was important to Tolkien because it represented the view of ordinary people he had held since his comradeship with the foot soldiers of the First World War. It was their loyalty, honesty, and simple-heartedness which he wanted to embody in Frodo Baggins' companion Sam Gamgee in *The Lord of the Rings.*

Here [in the story of Beren and Lúthien] we meet ... the first example of the motive (to become dominant in Hobbits) that the great policies of world history, "the wheels of the world", are often turned not by the Lords and Governors, even gods, but by the seemingly unknown and weak—owing to the secret life of creation.

(Carpenter, ed., *Letters:* 149)

Edith gave birth to their first son, John, in November 1917. She nearly died in childbirth. Tolkien was unable to get leave from the army base in order to be with her in Cheltenham, where she was lying in, until a week after the delivery. In 1918, when he was stationed at Penkridge army camp in Staffordshire, Edith traveled south with him, but when he was posted back to Hull, Edith, weary with nursing the baby and still bearing the pain of the difficult delivery, refused to move again. (Carpenter, *Tolkien:* 98)

The period of romance and war gave way to domesticity when Tolkien took the family to Oxford and joined the staff compiling the last parts of the Oxford English Dictionary. Edith was uncomfortable in Oxford. She was not an intellectual and did not share Tolkien's interests. Tolkien did not encourage her, too, either:

partly because he did not consider it to be a necessary part of her role as wife and mother, and partly because his attitude to her in courtship ... was not associated with his own intellectual life. Edith's role as a wife at Oxford, then, ought to have been twofold. She might have made their home into an inviting place for his colleagues to visit and she might have engaged in the rounds of visits with each other that constituted a significant part of the dons' wives' social activity. But she was shy, and the style and manner of Tolkien's friends or students who visited and of the Oxford wives intimidated and even frightened her, and she did neither.

(Carpenter, *Tolkien:* 153-4)

Towards the end of their first stay at Oxford, Edith became pregnant again, and Tolkien was offered a position at Leeds University as a Reader in English Language. When the term began in September 1920, he moved to Leeds by himself leaving Edith, John, and the new baby, Michael, in Oxford. He visited them weekends, until the beginning of 1921. Then Edith felt ready to move.

Edith found Leeds much more congenial than Oxford. There was less stuffiness, grandeur, and formality. Edith made friends with other wives, and with those of her husband's students who came by the house. They were the same working class students who impressed Tolkien with their diligence and earnestness. There were informal dances and at Christmas there were parties for the children at which the Vice-Chancellor of the university dressed up as Father Christmas. Tolkien's income was sufficient for him to buy a large house and to employ both a maid and a nurse for the children. (Carpenter, *Tolkien*: 155)

The move back to Oxford, when Tolkien was appointed Rawlinson and Bosworth Professor of Anglo-Saxon heralded the beginning of Tolkien's most fruitful period as both a teacher and a writer. It also introduced him into a circle of friends who were brilliant, receptive, and convivial. For Edith returning to Oxford ushered in a period of unhappiness and loneliness. From the start, the move was ill-omened for her. Tolkien had gone on ahead to Oxford and bought a house without her seeing it. When she did, she realized it was too small. John and Michael had caught ringworm from a public comb they had used when they went to have their pictures taken at a photography studio. The treatment they required was lengthy and costly. The boys did not like their new school in Oxford. Edith became pregnant again. Priscilla, their last child, was born in 1929. She was a gladness for them since they'd been hoping for a girl. The next year, Tolkien bought the house next door, larger and better suited to them. But it did not really make things better for Edith. The problem lay in Tolkien's idea of their roles, which had already shaped their relationship early on. Edith:

> began to feel that she was being ignored by Ronald. In terms of actual hours he was ... in the house a great deal: much of his teaching was done there, and he was not often out for more than one or two evenings a week. But it was really a matter of his affections. He was very loving and considerate to her, greatly concerned

about her health ... and solicitous about domestic matters. But she
could see that one side of him only came alive when he was in the
company of men of his own kind.

(Carpenter, Tolkien: 156)

Edith was lonely. As during their first stay in Oxford, she again
had few friends. Unlike the students who visited the house at
Leeds, the Oxford students made her feel uneasy. They did not
know what to say to her and she felt uncomfortable speaking to
them. For company, she had the children and the servants. She
became irritable and authoritarian, "demanding that meals be precisely on time, that the children eat up every scrap, and that
servants should perform their work impeccably." (Carpenter,
Tolkien: 156) Her unhappiness also translated into poor health.
She suffered from sever headaches which could keep her in bed all
day. The discrepancy in their situations also made Edith resentful
of her husband, and especially of his male friends. The fact that
Tolkien believed that "[i]n this fallen world the 'friendship' that
should be possible between all human beings, is virtually impossible between man and woman" (Carpenter, ed., *Letters:* 48) did
not help matters.

Tolkien's response to Edith's unhappiness during these years, at
times, was to fortify his own position and assert his own needs in
spite of her opposition. In a letter to Michael years later, full of
fatherly advice about the relation of the sexes, he wrote,

There are many things that a man feels are legitimate even though
they cause a fuss. Let him not lie about them to his wife or lover!
Cut them out—or if worth a fight: just insist. Such matters may
arise frequently—the glass of beer, the pipe, the non writing of letters, the other friend, etc., etc. If the other side's claims really are
unreasonable (as they are at times between the dearest lovers and
most loving married folk) they are much better met by above board
refusal and "fuss" than subterfuge.

(Carpenter, Tolkien: 157)

As dearly as he loved Edith, it seems, however, that Tolkien simply placed a higher value on men than on women, if he was speaking his true mind—which there is no reason to doubt he was—when he wrote to Michael that "it is their [women's] gift to be receptive, stimulated, fertilized (in many other matters than the physical) by the male. Every teacher knows that. How quickly an intelligent woman can be taught, grasp his ideas, see his point—and how (with rare exceptions) they can go no further, when they leave his hand, or when they cease to take a *personal* interest in *him*." With regard to courtly love, romantic love or even the veneration of the Virgin Mary, Tolkien warned his son that a man must not lose the sense of "women as they are ... companions in shipwreck not guiding stars." (Carpenter, ed., *Letters:* 49)

Religion also became a matter of contention between them because Edith had converted to Roman Catholicism for Tolkien's sake before they were married, not because of an inward prompting of her spirit, nor did she come to love the Church. She did not like going to church or participating in the sacraments, particularly confession, and she was not happy that Tolkien took the children to church. Humphrey Carpenter reports that things came to a head when Edith's:

> smouldering anger about church-going burst into fury; but at last after one such outburst in 1940 there was a true reconciliation between her and Ronald, in which she explained her feelings and even declared that she wished to resume the practice of her religion [Anglicanism].
>
> (Carpenter, *Tolkien:* 157)

After this, Edith apparently did not go to church regularly herself, but also no longer resented Tolkien's practice of Catholicism. She also did not abandon her Christian belief. She told Clyde Kilby, an American scholar who visited them and worked for a short time with Tolkien trying to put the parts of *The Silmarillion* together, that she had said prayers for Christopher's return to health when he was ill. (www.christianitytoday.com)

It seems that in significant ways, Edith and Tolkien lived separate lives despite their underlying love and care for each other and their shared concern for their children. They kept very different hours. Tolkien stayed up late at night writing. They slept, after Priscilla's birth, in separate bedrooms. According to Humphrey Carpenter, Edith "was not well acquainted with the details of his books and did not have a deep understanding of them," although she was not entirely cut off from his art. She was the first to whom he showed the short stories *Leaf by Niggle* and *Smith of Wootton Major*, and her approval encouraged his efforts. They also did have some friends in common. Humphrey Carpenter describes a visit to the Tolkien household as a divided experience. A guest often had to field two separate conversations, one with Tolkien perhaps on the etymology of place names and another with Edith concerning the children's health. (Carpenter, *Tolkien*: 158) They also sometimes took separate vacations. In August of 1955, for example Tolkien and Priscilla went to Italy, stopping in Assisi (where he was "staggered by the frescoes") (Carpenter, ed., *Letters*: 223) and Venice (which Tolkien said "seemed incredibly, elvishly lovely— like a dream of Old Gondor") while Edith "went on a Mediterranean cruise with three friends." (Carpenter, *Tolkien*: 222)

As the years went by Edith's health deteriorated, especially because of a rather crippling arthritis which at times threatened to force her into a wheel chair, but never did, and she continued to do all the cooking and most of the housework. Tolkien himself was "good with his hands" and could repair things around the house. (Carpenter, *Tolkien*: 246) In 1953, the Tolkiens moved from their house on Northmoor Road to one on Sandfield Road in the Oxford suburb of Headington where they stayed until 1968. For a number of years until then, Edith had been going to the Miramar Hotel in Bournemouth, an English seaside town, by herself. It was restful, she was taken care of, and she liked the people there. She was comfortable with them and they had common interests. Edith and her friends sat by the sea, spoke of their children and grandchildren over coffee after dinner, and watched the television news in the common room before going to bed. After a time, Tolkien also went on holidays to Bournemouth with her. Although it was lacking in the kind of male companionship and conversation he enjoyed, it was a change of scenery and a break from his work especially pleasant when he was stuck in his writing. He also saw that Edith was happier there than she had been over the course of the many years at Oxford. In 1968, Tolkien and Edith moved to a bungalow near Bournemouth. It was a delight for Edith, and that pleased him. There was a Roman Catholic Church nearby, and his next door neighbors were Roman Catholic and happy to drive him to church. Visitors did come to see him, but they were visitors he wanted to see. His Oxford address and telephone number were public. However his address and phone number in Bournemouth were kept private. He and Edith also often went to dine at the hotel and sometimes spent the night. They sat for many hours in their garden talking, he smoking his pipe, she, the cigarettes she had begun to smoke late in life. On the twenty-ninth of November, 1971, a Monday, Edith died at the age of eighty-two. In a letter to Christopher the next July, expressing the wish that "someone close in heart to me should know something about things that records do not record," Tolkien described the core of his and Edith's marriage:

> the dreadful sufferings of our childhoods, from which we rescued one another, but could not wholly heal the wounds that later often proved disabling; the sufferings that we endured after our love began—all of which (over and above our personal weaknesses) might help to make pardonable, or understandable, the lapses and darknesses which at times marred our lives—and to explain how these never touched our depths nor dimmed our memories of our youthful love. For ever (especially when alone) we still met in the woodland glade, and went hand in hand many times to escape the shadow of imminent death before our last parting.
>
> (Carpenter, ed., *Letters:* 420-1)

Tolkien's relationship with his children seems to have been warm, close, and, as seen by his letters to them, long-lasting. The children, too, seem to have been close to him and to have remained so even as adults. Each of their adult lives also shows how greatly influenced they were by him. The eldest John, who died in January 2003, became a Roman Catholic priest. Michael became a schoolmaster in a Jesuit school. His daughter, Priscilla, became a social worker. She has written about her parents' life in Staffordshire from 1916 to 1918, hosts meetings of the Tolkien Society and with her brother John put together *The Tolkien Family Album*, published in 1992. It was Christopher, the youngest boy, to whom Tolkien seems to have been closest. In fact, Tolkien fictionally portrayed his youngest son in the unfinished "The Lost Road." And, certainly, it was Christopher who was most profoundly influenced by his father's work. Indeed, he became not only his literary executor, but also edited the unfinished work and shaped it for publication after his father's death. He had followed that work, his father's evolving stories, with care since his childhood. Just how intently is shown by the following anecdote John and Priscilla tell in *The Tolkien Family Album*:

> Christopher was always much concerned with the consistency of the story and on one occasion ... interrupted: 'Last time, you said Bilbo's front door was blue, and you said Thorin had a golden tassel on this hood, but you've just said that Bilbo's front door was green, and the tassel on Thorin's hood was silver'; at which point Ronald exclaimed 'Damn the boy!' and strode across the room to make a note.
>
> (Tolkien, P and J. Tolkien: 58)

During Tolkien's lifetime, when Christopher returned to Oxford after being stationed in South Africa during the Second World War, he became part of his father's circle of male companions. As a regular member of the *Inklings*, it was he, Christopher, who read the group the new sections of *The Lord of the Rings*. Tolkien's reading was, by the group's opinion, inferior to his son's. Christopher also followed in his father's footsteps by becoming a don at Oxford. In 1958, Christopher delivered a paper at St. Anne's College on the differing ways Germanic poets and Roman writers described legendary northern heroes. It was called "Barbarians and Citizens." Tolkien was present and wrote the following letter to Christopher:

I think it was a very excellent performance. It filled me with great delight: first of all because it was so interesting to me that, after a day (for me) of unceasing labor and movement, I never desired to close my eyes or abstract my mind for a second—and I felt that all around me; and secondly because of paternal pride.

(Carpenter, ed., *Letters:* 264)

One small mark of Tolkien's pride in Christopher appears on a thank you note to Dr. Warfield M. Firor of Johns Hopkins University for the gift of a ham. In the years after the war food was scarce and there was rationing and many Americans sent "CARE" packages to Europe. "The undersigned, having just partaken of your ham, have drunk your health," it reads. It is signed by a number of people including Christopher Tolkien. J.R.R. Tolkien's is the last signature on the page. After his name, Tolkien identifies himself: M.A. Merton Professor of English Language and Literature, late Professor of Anglo-Saxon (Pembroke College) and exhibitioner of Exeter College, and of the Lancashire Fusiliers (1914–8) and father of the above C.R.T." (Carpenter, 144 facing)

In a piece he wrote for *The London Sunday Telegraph* in September of 1973, Tolkien's middle son, Michael, born at Oxford in 1920, remembers his father:

Inevitably he was not a super-human father, and often found his children insufferably irritating, self-opinionated, foolish and even occasionally totally incomprehensible. But he never lost his ability to talk to and not *at* or *down* to his children. In my own case he always made me feel that what I was doing and what I was thinking in my youth were of far more immediate importance than anything he was doing or thinking.

(Grotta-Kurska: 65)

Alluding to C.S. Lewis' remark that although he (Lewis) liked *The Hobbit*, he didn't know if a "modern child" would, Tolkien described how he related to children, saying,

I am not interested in the "child" as such, modern or otherwise, and certainly have no intention of meeting him/her half way, or a quarter of the way. It is a mistaken thing to do anyway, either use- less (when applied to the stupid) or pernicious (when inflicted on the gifted).

(Carpenter, *Tolkien:* 179)

The ability to communicate with children that Michael sug- gested his father possessed showed itself particularly in his ability to enter completely into their imaginative world. Perhaps as important, he did not exclude them from his. His daughter Priscilla recalled at the centenary of his birth:

He was always there, at lunch and at tea. We children were allowed to run in and out of his study at any time, so long as he wasn't actually teaching. He was very much involved with family life and, since we were often hard up, he had to write and work far into the night just to make extra money.

(27)

For his children and for the millions of readers throughout the world who later read his books, which partially began as stories to tell his children, (Carpenter, ed., *Letters:* 346) Tolkien was more than a storyteller. He created a world which seemed to contain, already made, the stories he told. When John, his firstborn, was three years old and Michael was a newborn, Tolkien began to create a fantasy world for them, which then yielded characters and incidents. Like many children, John hung up a stocking for Christmas and wrote a letter to Father Christmas telling him what he wanted. Tolkien, in the persona of Father Christmas wrote a letter back to him:

Dear John,

I heard you ask daddy what I was like & where I lived. I have drawn ME & My House for you. Take care of the picture. I am just off now for Oxford with my bundle of toys—some for you.

Hope I shall arrive in time: the snow is very thick at the NORTH POLE tonight:. Yr loving Fr. Chr.

(Tolkien, *Christmas Letters*)

Tolkien continued to write these letter for the next nineteen years until 1939, when he wrote to Christopher, who was fifteen then and Priscilla who was ten, the last letter, elegiac not just because the children were growing up and away from the fantasy but because war was on the horizon.

In the course of the nineteen years of his annual letter, the fiction developed. Tolkien created an entire *mise en scene* and a cast of characters including the North Polar Bear who was always getting into mischief and causing havoc but who was, nevertheless, lovable, and, in the end, fought heroically against the Goblins. The North Polar Bear had two nephews, rather like him in mischievousness, and Father Christmas got a secretary, Ilbereth, an elf, who also wrote to the children, sometimes in Elvish. Father Christmas, Ilbereth, and the North Polar Bear also sent pictures, and sometimes the actual Oxford postman colluded with Tolkien and actually delivered the letters to the house.

It was not only through the Father Christmas letters that his children contributed both to Tolkien's body of work and the movement of his imagination. While they were living at Leeds, John often could not fall asleep, and Tolkien told him stories of his own invention. Among them were the continuing adventures of Carrots, a red-haired boy "who climbed into a cuckoo clock and went off on a series of strange adventures." (Carpenter, *Tolkien*: 161) There were also tales of Bill Stickers and his adversary Major Road-Ahead. Their names were derived from street signs: the warning against posting, "Bill Stickers Will Be Prosecuted" and the traffic advisory, "Major Road Ahead." In 1925, during a summer holiday, Michael lost a stuffed dog on the beach. His grief at this loss generated a story his father made up to console him. It was about a dog named Rover who was turned into a stuffed dog by a wizard. Then he was lost by a small boy on the beach and found by a "sand-sorcerer," who restored Rover's ability to move and launched him on a trip to the moon. There, among his other adventures he had to deal with a dragon. (Carpenter, *Tolkien*: 162) The story became "Roverandom."

Tom Bombadil, who figures in *The Lord of the Rings* and who represents "the spirit of the (vanishing) Oxford and Berkshire countryside," also had his beginnings as an entertainment for the children. Tom Bombadil is in many ways a precursor hobbit, despite his boots—hobbits have furry feet and go unshod. He was "four foot high in his boots…and three feet broad. He wore a tall hat with a blue feather, his jacket was blue, and his boots were yellow." (Carpenter, *Tolkien*: 162) Tom Bombadil was modeled on a Dutch doll of Michael's, which John had stuffed down the toilet, from which Tolkien retrieved it. In another story, Tolkien used himself as the model for the protagonist. Mr Bliss buys a "bright yellow automobile for five shillings," and the story tells about his automotive adventures. Tolkien himself was a notoriously reckless driver who paid little attention to traffic signs or pedestrians, and was known to cry out as he drove heedless of what- or whoever was in his way, "Charge 'em and they scatter." (Carpenter, *Tolkien*: 159) The children also got to hear the beginnings of *The Hobbit* and *The Lord of the Rings*. Not long after *The Hobbit*'s publication in 1937, Christopher Tolkien wrote in his letter to Father Christmas,

> Daddy wrote it [*The Hobbit*] ages ago, and read it to John, Michael and me in our Winter "Reads" after tea in the evening; but the ending chapters were rather roughly done, and not typed out at all; he finished it about a year ago.
>
> (Carpenter, Tolkien: 177)

Tolkien felt an especial affinity with Christopher, of whom he wrote in his diary in the early 1930s that he was "a nervy, cross-grained, self-tormenting, cheeky person. Yet there is something intensely loveable about him, to me at any rate, from the very similarity between us." (Carpenter, *Tolkien*: 169) Often, in the early 1930s, Christopher would sit near the stove in his father's study while Tolkien told him the stories that were cohering at the time, even through these very tellings, into *The Lord of the Rings*. In the last days of the Second World War, when Christopher was stationed in South Africa, Tolkien sent him long letters discussing his work and confessing that "I don't think I should write any more, but for the hope of your seeing it." (Carpenter, ed., *Letters* 94)

CHAPTER SIX

Fellowship

The unpayable debt that I owe him was not "influence" as it is ordinarily understood, but sheer encouragement. He was for long my only audience. Only from him did I ever get the idea that my "stuff" could be more than a private hobby.

—Tolkien on C.S. Lewis (Carpenter, 32)

With C. S. Lewis, Tolkien enjoyed a deep friendship for nearly forty years, though they were not on close terms in the last ten leading up to Lewis' death. In October 1933, Tolkien wrote of him in his diary: "besides giving constant pleasure and comfort," friendship with Lewis

> has done me much good from the contact with a man at once honest, brave, intellectual—a scholar, a poet, a philosopher—and a lover, at least after a long pilgrimage, of Our Lord.
>
> (Carpenter, 52)

C. S. Lewis was undoubtedly as important in the development and composition of *The Lord of the Rings* as Tolkien's children, and especially Christopher. Since his days at King Edward's, fellowship was as necessary as family for Tolkien. It provided him with the companionship of men like himself, with whom he could converse, share interests, and, sometimes, form strong bonds. From his earliest school days, Tolkien was club-oriented. There was the T.C.B.S at King Edward's, important in itself but raised to an intensity of feeling by the slaughter of two of the original four in World War One. At Oxford during his first year, Tolkien formed *The Apolausticks,* a literary dining club. When he was teaching at Leeds, Tolkien formed *The Vikings.* He and E.V. Gordon, his colleague and collaborator on the edition of *Sir Gawain and the Green Knight,* gathered with students, read sagas, but also drank beer and enjoyed singing together. When he began teaching at Oxford, after the war, Tolkien founded the *Kolbitar,* Icelandic for coalbiters—people who sit around the fire so close on cold nights when they are talking together that they are near enough to bite the coals. It was "an informal reading club." (Carpenter, *Tolkien:* 120) Starting it was part of an effort to popularize the study of Icelandic in the English Studies department at Oxford. *The Coalbiters* gathered to read Icelandic sagas in the original, going around the circle and each reading and translating as much as he could, helped by Tolkien, who was fluent. The group was composed of illustrious members. Among them: George Gordon, then the President of Magdalen College; Nevill Coghill, a Chaucerian scholar noted for his translations of *The Canterbury Tales* and *Troilus and Cressida* into modern English; C.T. Onions, one of the editors of the Oxford English Dictionary; R.M. Dawkins, a professor of Byzantine and Modern Greek; and C.S. Lewis. In addition to the Coalbiters, Tolkien also belonged to *The Cave* and *The Oyster Club. The Cave* was formed to facilitate informal dinners. The members of *The Oyster* club gathered to celebrate the end of marking examinations by eating oysters.

It was the *Inklings,* however, which achieved fame as an extraordinary circle of exceptional, learned, conservative, Christian, romantic writers. It served as the incubator for a number of important works of literature which came out of England in the nineteen thirties, forties and fifties. The *Inklings* was, in its first incarnation, a literary society at Oxford founded by Edward Tangye Lean, an undergraduate and the editor of *Isis,* an Oxford

University magazine. Its purpose was to provide a place where the members could read their unpublished work to each other. Both Tolkien and Lewis were involved in it. When Lean left Oxford in 1933, Tolkien wrote later, Lewis appropriated the name for "the undetermined and unelected circle of friends who gathered about [him] and met in his rooms at Magdalen" or at a pub called *The Eagle and Child*, which they renamed *The Bird and Baby* because of its sign: the eagle Zeus carrying off the boy Ganeymede. Tolkien explained why they kept the name Inklings: "It was a pleasantly ingenious pun in its way, suggesting people with vague or half-formed intimations and ideas plus those who dabble in ink." (Carpenter, 67)

The *Inklings* was, in its way, the fulfillment of the T.C.B.S. Here was a band of men joined together to encourage in each other their greatest creativity and both individually and collectively to make their mark. Tolkien recalled, for example, the genesis of Lewis' novel, *Out of the Silent Planet*. In 1937, when Tolkien was reading the beginnings of *The Lord of the Rings* to the *Inklings*, trying to come up with a sequel to *The Hobbit*, "Lewis said to me…: 'Tollers, there is too little of what we really like in stories. I am afraid we shall have to write some ourselves." (Carpenter, 65–6) The novelist and poet, John Wain, who was then an undergraduate at Oxford began going to the *Inklings* on Thursday nights in the 1940s. Bad eyesight had kept him out of the Second World War and C. S. Lewis was his tutor. He wrote of the group: "This was a circle of instigators, almost of incendiaries, meeting to urge one another on in the task of redirecting the whole current of contemporary art and life." (Carpenter, 160) They especially opposed the liberal New Critical and reader-centered hermeneutics of critics like F.R. Leavis and I.A. Richards based in Cambridge. Leavis argued for "'culture' as the basis of a humane society," but did not think that culture ought to be "based on any one objective standard," and certainly not Christianity. Lewis saw Leavis and Richards as following in a "tradition of educated infidelity" going back to Matthew Arnold, which represented a "general rebellion against God." (Carpenter, 63–64)

It was a receptive environment for Tolkien. He first read *The

Hobbit to Lewis in manuscript form as he was composing it, and later parts of *The Lord of the Rings* to the *Inklings*. In letters to Christopher, he often reported how well Lewis and the *Inklings* received them. Carpenter notes that there were those in the circle who were not entirely drawn into the fantasy world, however. Hugo Dyson, a lecturer in English at Reading University and later a Fellow and Tutor in English Literature at Merton College, Oxford, for example, was not an enthusiast (Carpenter, 212–13) and reportedly quipped, adding a strong obscenity during one of Tolkien's readings, "Oh ... not another elf." (Wilson: 217) Among the *Inklings*, however, Tolkien was not only the bearer of his own work but he was midwife to C.S. Lewis's. Tolkien's imaginative universe suggested a similar one to Lewis, and they stimulated each other with encouragement and ideas.

Lewis' tale of space travel, *Out of the Silent Planet,* was not only directly the result of a conversation with Tolkien, but after Lewis' own publisher, J.M. Dent rejected the book, Stanley Unwin of Allen & Unwin—publishers of *The Hobbit*—sent a reader's report on *Silent Planet* to Tolkien, who responded:

> I read the story in the original; MS., and was so enthralled that I could do nothing else until I had finished it. My first criticism was simply that it was too short. I still think that criticism holds, for both practical and artistic reasons. Other criticisms, concerning narrative style (Lewis is always apt to have rather creaking stiff-jointed passages), inconsistent details in the plot, and philology, have since been corrected to my satisfaction.... I ... should have bought this story at almost any price if I had found it in print.
>
> (Carpenter, 66)

The readers at Allen & Unwin did not agree with Tolkien, but Stanley Unwin did, and he was also chairman of The Bodley Head Press, which published *Out of the Silent Planet* in the fall of 1938. In 1943, Lewis published a sequel to *Out of the Silent Planet* called *Perelandra,* of which Tolkien also thought very highly. In both novels, as Tolkien's daughter Priscilla noticed, the character Ransom, a philologist seems to have been modeled after Tolkien, and Tolkien, himself, acknowledged his part in the character: "As a philologist, I may have some part in him, and recognize some of my opinions and ideas Lewisified in him." Ransom's first name is "Elwin," or elf-friend, from the old English *Aelfwine*. (Carpenter, 182) Lewis' books of Christian apologetics, too, like *The Four Friendships*, derive from his friendship with Tolkien, and Lewis dedicated *The Screwtape Letters* to Tolkien. But Tolkien did not like that book, nor did he like the books which together make up the children's series, *The Chronicles of Narnia*, the first of which is *The Lion, the Witch, and the Wardrobe*.

While never disavowing their friendship, Tolkien and Lewis, by the late 1940s, were growing distant from each other. Beside Tolkien's reservations about some of Lewis' literary work, the fact that Lewis professed Anglicanism rather than Roman Catholicism, even though Tolkien took joy in Lewis' return to Christianity, unsettled him, especially because he detected a strain of bias against Roman Catholicism in Lewis. Apparently, there was a certain amount of jealousy on Tolkien's part, too, jealousy of Lewis' friendship with Charles Williams and, later, in the fifties, of Lewis' late-in-life marriage to Joy Davidman Gresham, which also destabilized the friendship. Tolkien said as much himself in a 1964 letter:

> Yes C. S. L. was my closest friend from about 1927 to 1940, and remained very dear to me. His death [on November 22, 1963, the same day as the assassination of John Kennedy] was a grievous blow. But in fact we saw less and less of one another after he came under the dominant influence of Charles Williams, and still less after his very strange marriage.
>
> (Carpenter, ed., *Letters:* 349)

Whether C.S. Lewis' marriage to Joy Gresham was "very strange" is not an issue necessary to consider in an essay exploring Tolkien's life, but the reasons it could prove disturbing to him provide insight into his character and values. Gresham was a Jewish convert to Christianity, a Protestant, like Lewis, not a Roman Catholic, and she had been divorced. For Tolkien "[t]oleration of divorce ... is toleration of a human abuse." (Carpenter, ed., *Letters*: 61) His thoughts on this point were not published until *The Letters of J.R.R. Tolkien* appeared. Even, however, without Tolkien's doctrinal beliefs about divorce, Lewis' marriage would have had something unpalatable for several other, purported secular reasons. One was that Tolkien learned of the marriage only by reading about it in *The Times*. Another was that for all the years of their friendship, Lewis had kept the *Inklings* an all male association and Lewis "had expressed little or no interest in Tolkien's family life or troubles and insisted that" Tolkien and the others "should come out alone to the gatherings." Now that he was married and his perspective altered, he wanted Joy to be part of the group. (Wilson: 271) Many Tolkien scholars are doubtful of this view, because Lewis most likely would not have considered inviting Joy to join the all-male club. Even though Lewis' marriage secured the distance between him and Tolkien, Joy Lewis and Edith Tolkien eventually became friends.

Charles Williams was a poet, a novelist, a playwright, and an essayist who published more than forty books. He worked at the Oxford University Press as the assistant to Humphrey Milford, the publisher. He taught evening classes at the City Literary Institute and the Evening Institutes run by the London County Council, lecturing on English literature, and specializing in Milton, Shakespeare, and Wordsworth. He had a brilliance and energy which fascinated C.S. Lewis. Significantly, too, his own writing, although often set in familiar English locations and written in a conventional genre, for example, the detective story, like his first novel, *War in Heaven*, involved fantasy and the fundamental religious theme of the struggle between divine and demonic forces. (Carpenter, 73ff.)

Lewis and Williams met each other in 1936 through their writing. Both R. W. Chambers, Professor of Literature at London University, and Nevill Coghill, at Exeter, recommended Williams' novel *The Place of the Lion* to Lewis. After reading it, Lewis wrote to his friend, Arthur Greeves, to whom he had praised Tolkien's "Lay of Leithian" so strongly, "I have just read what I think a really great book.... It isn't often nowadays you get a *Christian* fantasy."

(Carpenter, 99) At the same time that Lewis was reading William's novel, Williams, as part of his job at Oxford University Press was reading the page proofs of Lewis' forthcoming *The Allegory of Love* in order to write a descriptive paragraph of it for the Sales Department. Williams was as taken with Lewis' book as Lewis had been with Williams'. Lewis was in the habit of writing to authors whose books he admired, and, accordingly, in March 1936, he wrote to Williams, who wrote back: "If you had delayed writing another 24 hours our letters would have crossed. It has never before happened to me to be admiring an author of a book while he at the same time was admiring me…. You must be in London sometimes. Do let me know and come and have lunch or dinner." (Carpenter, 99-100) In 1939, at the start of the war, the London staff of the Oxford University Press was evacuated to Oxford. In this way, William's association with Lewis was strengthened, and he became a regular member of the *Inklings*. More distressing to Tolkien than William's presence at the gatherings of the *Inklings* was the fact that Williams began to intrude directly (from Tolkien's point of view) on his friendship with Lewis. He began to join them regularly at their Monday morning talks at the Eastgate Hotel pub over a pint. This had been a private ritual which Tolkien and Lewis had been enjoying for more than ten years, and Williams' presence changed the feel of the event and the nature of the conversation. (Carpenter, 121)

From the letters, journal entries, and marginalia available, Tolkien seems to have been of several minds about Charles Williams. Perhaps his ambivalence is most clearly demonstrated by comparing two of his letters. In 1965, in a letter to Dick Plotz of the Tolkien Society of America, Tolkien contrasted his own mythology with C.S. Lewis', explaining that Lewis':

> mythology (incipient and never fully realized) was quite different. It was at any rate broken to bits before it became coherent by contact with C.S. Williams and his "Arthurian" stuff—which happened between *Perelandra* and *That Hideous Strength*. A pity, I think. But then I was and remain wholly unsympathetic to Williams' mind.

From this remark, Tolkien proceeded to discuss Williams himself:

> I knew Charles Williams only as a friend of C.S.L., whom I met in his company when, owing to the War, he spent much of his time in Oxford. We liked one another and enjoyed talking (mostly in jest) but we had nothing to say to one another at deeper (or higher) levels. I doubt if he had read anything of mine then available; I had read or heard a good deal of his work but found it totally alien, and sometimes very distasteful, occasionally ridiculous.

As he usually did when he passed what may be taken for a negative judgment, Tolkien concluded by taking the fault upon himself rather than burdening the object of his criticism with it, and then found something complimentary to say:

> (This is perfectly true as a general statement, but is not intended as a criticism of Williams; rather it is an exhibition of my own limits of sympathy. And of course in so large a range of work I found lines, passages, scenes, and thoughts that I found striking.)
>
> (Carpenter, ed., *Letters:* 361–362)

Writing to Williams' widow in 1945, on the day after Williams' death, however, Tolkien said: "in the (far too brief) years since I first met him I had grown to admire and love your husband deeply." (Carpenter, ed., Letters: 115) But in his edition of the *Essays presented to Charles Williams,* published in 1947, in the margins of C.S. Lewis' tribute, next to Lewis' assertion that by 1939 Williams "had already become as dear to all my Oxford friends as he had to me," Tolkien wrote, "Alas no!" (Carpenter, 120) In a letter responding to a reader's fan mail, Tolkien expressed both aspects of his own relationship to Williams:

> (...) We both listened ... to large and largely unintelligible fragments of one another's works read aloud; because C.S.L. (marvelous man) seemed able to enjoy us both. But I think we both found the other's mind (or rather mode of expression, and cli-

mate) as impenetrable when cast into "literature", as we found the other's presence and conversation delightful.

(Carpenter, ed., Letters: 209)

Edith Tolkien's resentment of Ronald's male friendships was focused particularly on his friendship with C.S. Lewis. Lewis was uncomfortable with her, and spoke of a woman's inability to converse on intellectual topics:

> The men have learned to live among ideas. They know what discussion, proof, and illustration mean. A woman who has had merely school lessons and has abandoned soon after marriage whatever tinge of "culture" they gave her—whose reading is the Women's Magazines and whose general conversation is almost wholly narrative—cannot really enter such a circle [of male friends]. If the men are ruthless, she sits bored and silent through a conversation which means nothing to her. If they are better bred, of course, they try to bring her in. Things are explained to her: people try to sublimate her irrelevant and blundering observations into some kind of sense. But the efforts soon fail.

(Carpenter, 165)

It does not strain the imagination to see why she resented her husband's alliance with Lewis or why she was put off by him. Besides his desire to exclude his male friends' wives from his social engagement with them, when Lewis visited the Tolkien household, Humphrey Carpenter reports, Lewis was shy and uncommunicative with Edith, although he spoke freely with the children and brought them books. It was at the time when Edith's resentment of Roman Catholicism and of how Tolkien kept an important part of himself separate from her was a source of domestic strife. She was accurate in her assessment, for a vital part of her husband that was essentially closed to her opened to Lewis. And even in Tolkien's mind, his wife and his friend seemed to be in inverse relation to each other: Tolkien wrote in his diary "Friendship with Lewis compensates for much." (Carpenter, 32)

Tolkien and Lewis became acquainted on May 11, 1926. C.S. Lewis recorded the event in his diary:

Tolkien managed to get the discussion round to the proposed English Prelim. I had a talk with him afterwards. He is a smooth, pale, fluent little chap—can't read Spenser because of the forms—thinks the language is the real thing in the school—thinks all literature is written for the amusement of *men* between thirty and forty—we ought to vote ourselves out of existence if we were honest—still the sound changes and the gobbets are great fun for the dons. His pet abomination is the idea of "liberal studies". Technical hobbies are more in his line. No harm in him: only needs a smack or so.

(Carpenter, 22)

They met at an English Department tea where Tolkien introduced his proposal—which finally passed in 1931—for changing course requirements and paying more attention to the study of northern and medieval languages and linguistics and to pre-Chaucerian literature. Soon after, Tolkien invited Lewis to join the Coalbiters, and by January 1927, he was attending meetings, reading Icelandic sagas and learning Icelandic. The experience made him more inclined to support Tolkien's proposed change in the English Department curriculum, which was just what Tolkien undoubtedly expected it to do. Most significantly, however, it brought him in contact with Tolkien, with a man who shared many of the same interests and ways of seeing things as himself. That mutuality of interest cemented a bond between them. In a letter dated December 3, 1929 to his friend Arthur Greeves, Lewis wrote:

I was up till 2.30 on Monday, talking to the Anglo-Saxon professor Tolkien, who came back with me to the College from a society and sat discoursing of the gods and giants of Asgard for three hours, then departing in the wind and rain—who could turn him out, for the fire was bright and the talk good.

(Carpenter, 28)

Soon after this conversation Tolkien gave Lewis a copy of his poem, "The Gest of Beren and Lúthien," as yet unfinished. It was a rather unusual thing for Tolkien to do, for, according to Humphrey Carpenter, Tolkien did not show others the long poems he was working on. A harsh critical response to some poetry he had sent to a former teacher made him reluctant to show his work to others. He was moved to trust Lewis, however. In him he found a man with similar interests, especially a love of Northern fairy stories and heroic tales. In his youth, Lewis, too, had delighted in William Morris' Icelandic translations and imitations and had himself written pastiches modeled on Norse poetry and drama. A few days later, Lewis wrote to Tolkien:

> Just a line to say that I sat up late last night and read the geste as far as to where Beren and his gnomish allies defeat the patrol of the orcs above the sources of the Narog and disguise themselves in the reaf. I can quite honestly say that it is ages since I have had an evening of such delight: and the personal interest of reading a friend's work had very little to do with it—I should have enjoyed it just as well if I'd picked it up in a bookshop, by an unknown author. The two things that come out clearly are the sense of reality in the background and the mythical value: the essence of a myth being that it should *suggest* incipient allegories to the reader. So much at the first flush. Detailed criticisms (including grumbles at individual lines) will follow.
>
> (Carpenter, 30)

What did follow was a long, detailed criticism couched as a scholarly edition of the text as if it were an ancient manuscript with annotations by several scholars called variously "Peabody," "Pumpernickel," Bentley," and "Schick." Lines he did not like, Lewis' personae concluded, were the results of textual corruption and errors at the hands of copyists. Lewis also rewrote many passages, changing the verses considerably.

Tolkien rejected many of Lewis' criticisms and emendations. The two, as poets and as thinkers were quite different from each other. Lewis wrote a verse that was stronger and more literary than Tolkien's. Carpenter calls it metrically assured and philosophically complex. Tolkien's verse could tend to slackness. His was a plain style that showed little literary influence but went about the business of narrative using the tools of poetry and poetic language

Tolkien had gathered in his philological work. When Lewis recommended replacing Tolkien's lines, "Hateful thou art, O Land of Trees!/ My flute shall fingers no more seize," with "Oh, hateful land of trees, be mute!/ My fingers, now forget the flute," Tolkien rejected it as "Frightful 18th century!!!" (Carpenter, 31) But Tolkien also took much of Lewis' criticism seriously and made extensive revisions or entirely rewrote sections in response to it. Lewis remarked that Tolkien "has only two reactions to criticism. Either he begins the whole work over again from the beginning or else takes no notice at all." (Carpenter, *Tolkien*: 145) The enthusiasm that Lewis showed encouraged Tolkien, and Tolkien began reading him large portions of *The Silmarillion*, and let him review the near-completed *Hobbit* manuscript.

C.S. Lewis wrote in his autobiography, *Surprised by Joy*, that his friendship with Tolkien:

> marked the breakdown of two old prejudices. At my first coming into the world I had been (implicitly) warned never to trust a Papist, and at my first coming into the English faculty (explicitly) never to trust a philologist. Tolkien was both.
>
> (Lewis: 216)

Lewis overcame one prejudice by seeing, through both his conversations with Tolkien and the meetings of the Coalbiters, that Tolkien was as deeply in love with Northern literature as he was. But religion, too, was as important as literature to both of them. They were especially concerned, in their conversations, with problems of belief and how we know something. Even after they had recognized their common stand regarding literature, even after Lewis realized the Tolkien as a philologist was not a dry-as-dust pedant who stripped the joy from its study, Lewis still could not accept Tolkien's Christianity. He was especially unable to accept Tolkien's fundamental belief in the reality of a Divine Christ. Their dialogue on religion, which ultimately brought Lewis to Tolkien's position even if not to his Church, nevertheless involved literature as much as theology. Indeed, for both of them there was not a clear line of demarcation separating literature and religion.

What joined them was mythology. The contention between Tolkien and Lewis involved understanding just what mythology was. Lewis saw mythology as a kind of lie. Tolkien understood it as a means of representing truth.

Lewis had been brought up in the Church of Ireland an Anglican Protestant. During adolescence, he became an atheist. In his late twenties, he gave up atheism. He reasoned there must be "some sort of God," to account for the existence of everything, denying, however, the possibility of absolute knowledge. (Carpenter, 39) Lewis' concern was with rationality, with discovering a belief in God that did not violate intellectual understanding, his "bow wow dogmatism," Lewis called it. (Carpenter, 35) His journey towards Christianity depended upon his becoming aware of the authenticity of the imaginative. He was not out of touch with emotional experience; he simply did not credit it. "Imaginative vision," he argued to his friend Owen Barfield, "cannot be invoked as a source of certainty—for any one judgement against another." (Carpenter, 37) This position led him to postulate and believe in the existence of a Hegelian "absolute," rather than an incarnate deity. (Carpenter, 39) Tolkien's position was quite the opposite. He had no doubt about the truth of Christianity or the divine person of Jesus Christ. It was rooted in him not primarily by intellectual argument but by its connection with his mother, by his love for her, and by her suffering because of her religious devotion. Tolkien made it very clear in a letter he wrote to Michael in January 1965:

> When I think of my mother's death ... worn out with persecution, poverty, and, largely consequent, disease, in the effort to hand on to us small boys the Faith, and remember the tiny bedroom she shared with us in rented rooms in a postman's cottage at Rednal, where she died alone, too ill for viaticum, I find it very hard and bitter, when my children stray away [from the Catholic Faith].
>
> (Carpenter, ed., *Letters:* 353–4)

The turning point for Lewis came on September 19, 1931, when he invited Tolkien and their friend Hugo Dysen, a lecturer in English at Reading University and a member of the Church of England, to dine with him in his rooms at Magdalen College. It was Tolkien's explanation of what mythology was and how it worked that facilitated Lewis' acceptance of Christianity. It is also fundamental for understanding Tolkien's vision of truth and his idea of what his own work as the writer-to-be of *The Hobbit* and *The Lord of the Rings* was about.

After dinner, Tolkien, Dyson, and Lewis walked through the grounds of Magdalen College. The argument was whether myths were true or not and what made them true or not. Lewis believed that myths were "lies and therefore worthless, even though breathed through silver." (Carpenter, 43) They are fictions with the capacity to provoke our responses, emotional and intellectual in a real way. But at their center, they offered nothing. Tolkien could agree that myths provoked deep and true responses in us, but he did not believe that myths are lies. Philologist that he was, he had a declension: God created man in His Own image. Being created in God's image man's ideas and ideals, even when he perverts them, are reflections of God. Lewis agreed with that. Tolkien continued. We, mankind, and the world we inhabit are "imaginative inventions" (Carpenter, 43) of God. One of our capacities therefore is also making "imaginative inventions." In "On Fairy-Stories," Tolkien called this "sub-creation." God is the Creator. Man is the sub-creator. His creations, even when corrupt, are likewise, therefore, made in the image of God. Sub-creations, thus, come from The Creator, diluted by coming through us but possessing some truth, because their origin is in God. That's why pagan stories have value as vehicles of partial truth.

Back in Lewis' rooms Tolkien, Dyson, and C.S. Lewis continued their conversation, centering on the central image of Christianity, the Crucified Christ. Lewis was split, as Humphrey Carpenter presents it, between the question, "how the life and death of Someone Else (whoever he was) two thousand years ago could help us here and now—except in so far as his example could help us," and his fascination with the crucifixion itself: "Right in the center, in the Gospels and in St. Paul, you keep on getting something quite different and very mysterious, expressed in those phrases I have so often ridiculed—'propitiation'—'sacrifice'—'the blood of the Lamb.'" He had found them, according to Humphrey Carpenter, "silly, shocking and meaningless."

Carpenter hypothesizes the rest of the conversation between them. Tolkien, he imagines, argues that "pagan myths were…God expressing himself through the minds of poets, and using the images of their "mythopoeia" [capacity for making mythic poetry] to express fragments of his eternal truth." Furthermore, he has Tolkien assert that "Christianity is exactly the same thing—with the enormous difference that the poet who invented it was God Himself, and the images He used were real men and actual history." (Carpenter, 44)

Tolkien's argument is a perfect justification of the kind of work he is devoted to, creating interconnected languages and stories of mythic proportion. The argument also lets readers of his epic understand that while his work does not carry an overt Christianized message, its very existence is a reflection of the Creator's work, through this act of sub-creation. In this way his work is a tribute to the Creator. Tolkien's final point illuminates, too, his sense of the effect myth has on the reader. The bond that formed between Tolkien and Lewis was based on a shared belief that myth is a valuable narrative mode because it reconstitutes primary images, actions, and relationships. Myth thus represents a recreation or a sub-creation of the Divine Creation and consequently is a vehicle for conveying Divine Truth. Tolkien and Lewis shared not just a common belief but consequently also a common purpose, to write mythic literature.

SEVEN

Authorship

I am in fact a hobbit in all but size. I like gardens,
trees, and unmechanized farmlands; I smoke a pipe,
and like good plain food (unrefrigerated), but detest
French cooking; I like, and even dare to wear in
these dull days, ornamental waistcoats. I am fond of
mushrooms (out of a field); have a very simple sense
of humour (which even my appreciative critics find
tiresome); I go to bed late and get up late (when pos-
sible). I do not travel very much.
        —Tolkien (Rogers, D. and I. Rogers: 126)

PHILOLOGIST OF LANGUAGES both real and of his own invention,
mythographer, storyteller, poet, moralist, antiquarian, devotee of
dragons, and lover of the vanishing English pastoral landscape—
all these aspects of Tolkien converged in *The Hobbit* and in *The
Lord of the Rings*. "One writes such a story out of the leaf-mould of
the mind," Tolkien remarked. (Carpenter, *Tolkien*: 178) Exactly
when Tolkien began composing *The Hobbit* is unsure. Even
Tolkien and his older children could not say the exact year of its
origin. Certainly, before he ever put pen to paper something of
The Hobbit existed as part of the domestic oral tradition of the
Tolkien family, for he told the children stories and developed them

as he told them. Tolkien did recall, however, *how* he began *writing* it and under what circumstances. It was during the summer, probably in 1930. In June 1955, he wrote to W. H. Auden that he thought of the idea while correcting school papers, and it became *The Hobbit* in the early 1930s:

> [The Hobbit] was eventually published not because of my own children's enthusiasm (though they liked it well enough), but because I lent it to the then Rev. Mother of Cherwell Edge when she had flu, and it was seen by a former student who was a that time in the office of Allen and Unwin. It was tried out on Rayner Unwin; but for whom when grown up I think I should never have got the Trilogy published.
>
> (Carpenter, ed., *Letters:* 215)

Humphrey Carpenter reports that Tolkien also remarked that after writing the sentence "In a hole in the ground there lived a hobbit": "Names always generate a story in my mind. Eventually I thought I'd better find out what hobbits were like. (Carpenter, *Tolkien:* 172)

In *The Hobbit*, using the character of Bilbo Baggins, Tolkien introduced a fairy tale version of himself into a countryside he called the Shire, which was a fairy tale version of the landscape of his childhood, Sarehole. And then he set a plot in motion which propelled him from the simple pleasures of English countryside contentment into the world of the medieval heroic epic, into the world of war, and into a world where the languages he invented became the actual languages of peoples and places.

By 1933, we know that Tolkien had written much of *The Hobbit* because there is a letter dated 4 February of that year, which C.S. Lewis wrote to his friend Arthur Greaves, "Since term began I have had a delightful time reading a children's story which Tolkien has just written…. Whether it is really *good* is of course another question; still more, whether it will succeed with modern children." (Carpenter, 57) But Tolkien was not really interested in succeeding with children "modern or otherwise" (Carpenter, ed., *Letters:* 309) He wrote his stories for himself. (Carpenter, ed., *Letters:* 412) He told them to his children, just as any parent makes up stories and tells them to the children but, he was not, of course, "any parent," but a professor of philology and a writer. He wrote for himself, but he undoubtedly wanted what he wrote to have a career in the world. He showed it, after all, to Lewis and to the Rev. Mother of Cherwell Edge. And it seems without an external demand for his work, it hovered without fulfilling itself. The manuscript Tolkien gave Lewis was a rough copy; it lacked an ending. (Carpenter, 57) Christopher Tolkien noted the same thing in his 1937 letter to Father Christmas: "the ending chapters were rather roughly done, and not typed out at all." (Carpenter, *Tolkien*: 177) Tolkien put it away in his study, occasionally showed it to a friend, but otherwise, it seemed to have become a souvenir of his children's period of growing up, like the letters from Father Christmas or the stories about Carrots, Bill Stickers or Michael's lost stuffed dog. That was until 1936, when outside forces intervened.

One of the few people Tolkien had shown the unfinished manuscript of *The Hobbit* to was Elaine Griffiths. She had been one of Tolkien's students, and had become a friend of the family. After graduation from Oxford she got a job in London, at Tolkien's recommendation, with the publishing firm of Allen & Unwin revising a translation of *Beowulf.* There she met another Oxford graduate who had studied English, Susan Dagnall. When Dagnall came down to Oxford to see Griffiths on business for Allen & Unwin, Griffiths told her about *The Hobbit* typescript and suggested she visit Tolkien and ask to borrow it. Griffiths had seen it because she had been "a student resident" at the house over which the Mother Superior of Cherwell Edge presided. Tolkien lent it to Dagnall, and she took it back to London. Susan Dagnall, after reading it, sent *The Hobbit* back to Tolkien and asked him to finish it so that it could be considered for publication during the next year. (Carpenter, *Tolkien*: 180) It was all he needed to set him working on it again. By October 1936, *The Hobbit* was finished and back at Allen & Unwin's. Stanley Unwin, the chairman of the company then put the book to the test by giving it to his ten year old son Rayner to read and then write a short review of it. He was paid a shilling, slight pay for such an important decision for the firm, but he later succeeded to the chairmanship and was responsible for the publication of *The Lord of the Rings*. Rayner wrote:

> Bilbo Baggins was a hobbit who lived in his hobbit-hole and never went for adventures, at last Gandalf the wizard and his dwarves perswaded [*sic*] him to go. He had a very exciting time fighting goblins and wargs. at [*sic*] last they got to a lonely mountain; Smaug, the dragon who gawreds [*sic*] it is killed and after a terrific battle with the goblins he returned home—rich! This book, with the help of maps, does not need illustrations it is good and should appeal to all children between the ages of 5 and 9.
>
> (Carpenter, *Tolkien:* 180-1)

Rayner's judgment was accepted, except in the matter of illustrations. Tolkien was asked for some, and, typically, wrote to the publisher: "The pictures seem to me mostly only to prove that the author cannot draw." (Carpenter, ed., *Letters:* 15) Eight of his black and white illustrations were used.

The Hobbit was published in September 1937 by Allen & Unwin. In a letter, Tolkien suggested why that might not be a good time for publication in terms of sales:

> I cannot help thinking that you are possibly mistaken in taking Oxford University and its terms into account; and, alternatively, if you do, in considering early October better than June. Most of O.U. will take no interest in such a story.... In any case late June … is a quiescent interlude, when light reading is sought, for immediate use and for vacation. October with the inrush of a new academic year is most distracted.
>
> (Carpenter, ed., *Letters:* 18)

But there was more:

> I have only one personal motive in regretting the delay [and waiting until October to publish *The Hobbit*]: and that is that I was anxious that it should appear as soon as possible, because I am under research-contract since last October, and not supposed to be

indulging in exams or in "frivolities". The further we advance into my contract time, the more difficulty I shall have (and I have already had some) in pretending that the work belongs wholly to the period before October 1936. I shall now find it very hard to make people believe that this is not the major fruits of "research." 1936-7!

(Carpenter, ed., *Letters:* 18-19)

Seeing himself the subject of dust-jacket advertising copy— "J.R.R. Tolkien has four children and *The Hobbit* ... was read to them in nursery days.... The manuscript ... was lent to friends in Oxford and read to their children..."—Tolkien characteristically commented that his children never had a nursery; that he read to them in his study; that his manuscript never was "read *to* children" of his friends. They read it themselves. Responding to further jacket copy describing him as "a professor of an abstruse subject at play," he said that he did not consider the study of Anglo-Saxon abstruse or the language remote. He added that "a professor at play rather suggests an elephant in its bath." (Carpenter, ed., *Letters:* 22) Finally he explained that if the jacket prose must compare him to Lewis Carroll, mention of *Through the Looking Glass* would be much more appropriate than of *Alice in Wonderland*.

C. S. Lewis was one of the principal reviewers of *The Hobbit* when it was published, with two reviews, one in *The Times* (of London) and one in *The Times Literary Supplement*. The reviews were enthusiastic: "All who love that kind of children's book," Lewis wrote, "which can be read and reread by adults should take note that a new star has appeared in this constellation." (Carpenter, *Tolkien:* 182) *The Hobbit* sold out before the beginning of Christmas. Stanley Unwin wrote Tolkien, "It is seldom that a children's writer gets firmly established with one book, but that you will do so very rapidly I have not the slightest doubt." (Carpenter, ed., *Letters:* 25) Tolkien learned in another letter from his publisher that a second printing was rushed through. "At the last minute the crisis was so acute that we fetched part of the reprint from our printers at Woking in a private car." (Carpenter, ed., *Letters:* 27)

When *The Hobbit* was published soon after in the United

States, it won the *New York Herald Tribune* prize for Best Children's Book of the Year and Tolkien got $250.00. Stanley Unwin wrote to Tolkien, "A large public will be clamouring next year to hear more from you about Hobbits!" (Carpenter, *Tolkien*: 182)

Tolkien had quite a few other manuscripts to show Unwin, "Mr. Bliss," "Farmer Giles of Ham," "Roverandom," and an unfinished novel called "The Lost Road" which he had begun at the time he and C.S. Lewis decided to write fantasy novels. "The Lost Road" set out to be a story of time travel, but Tolkien did not go far with it. The other book that Tolkien showed Unwin was *The Silmarillion*, disorganized and unfinished.

Allen & Unwin's expressed liking for the stories, but there were no hobbits in them. The publisher's response to *The Silmarillion* was more complex. The firm's reader did not like most of *The Silmarillion* at all. The Beren and Lúthien section was an exception. The original verse telling was unfinished, but there was a complete prose version. Of it the reader said:

> The tale here proceeds at a stinging pace. It is told with a picturesque brevity and dignity that holds the reader's interest in spite of its eye-splitting Celtic names. It has something of that mad, bright-eyed beauty that perplexes all Anglo-Saxons in face of Celtic art.
>
> (Carpenter, *Tolkien:* 184)

In a letter to Tolkien in December of 1937, Stanley Unwin included the reader's praise. He went on to express his own high regard for *The Silmarillion*. He said he thought of it as a "mine to be explored in writing further books like *The Hobbit* rather than a book in itself." He added, "I think this was partly your own view, was it not?" It was not! Tolkien very much wanted to see *The Silmarillion* published as a book, and a commission would have given him the impulse to finish it, as it did when Susan Dagnall spoke of accepting *The Hobbit*.

"What we badly need," Unwin continued, "is another book to follow up our success with *The Hobbit*." That was not *The Silmarillion*.

Tolkien understood that, as his reply clearly shows. First he dealt with the reaction to his books:

> My chief joy comes from learning that the Silmarillion is not rejected with scorn. I have suffered a sense of fear and bereavement, quite ridiculous, since I let this private and beloved manuscript out; and I think if it had seemed to you nonsense I should have felt really crushed.... But I shall certainly now hope one day to be able, or to be able to afford, to publish the Silmarillion. Your reader's comment affords me delight.
>
> (Carpenter, ed., *Letters:* 26)

Then he began thinking out loud about a work that would become *The Lord of the Rings:*

> I did not think any of the stuff I dropped on you filled the bill. But I did want to know whether any of the stuff had any exterior non-personal value. I think it is plain that quite apart from it, a sequel or successor to *The Hobbit* is called for.... And what more can hobbits do? They can be comic, but their comedy is suburban unless it is set against things more elemental. But the real fun about orcs and dragons (to my mind) was before their time. Perhaps a new (if similar) line? Do you think Tom Bombadil, the spirit of the (vanishing) Oxford and Berkshire countryside could be made into the hero of a story?
>
> (Carpenter, ed., *Letters:* 27)

A few days later, Tolkien wrote to his publishers to say that he had written "the first chapter of a new story about Hobbits—'A long expected party.'" (Carpenter, ed., *Letters:* 27) And in February he wrote to "ask Mr. Unwin whether his son ... would care to read the first chapter of the sequel to *The Hobbit*[.]" (Carpenter, ed., *Letters:* 28) Stanley Unwin wrote back to say that Rayner "was delighted with the first chapter." (Carpenter, ed., *Letters:* 29) Tolkien continued to send chapters to Rayner and to show them to C.S. Lewis. In a later letter to Allen & Unwin's, commenting on Rayner's objection to too much "hobbit talk" in the second and third chapters, Tolkien noted that Rayner's criticism "agrees strikingly with Mr. Lewis', which is therefore confirmed. I must plainly bow to my two chief (and most well-disposed) critics. The trouble is," he adds, "that 'hobbit talk' amuses me privately (and to a certain degree also my boy Christopher) more than adventures." (Carpenter, ed., *Letters*: 36) Soon, however, he was getting stuck. He wrote to C.A. Furth, an editor at Allen & Unwin in July 1938, elaborately on the problems he was having developing a sequel.

What Tolkien found was happening was not that he was moving outside *The Silmarillion*, but that he was bringing *The Silmarillion* inside the hobbit sequel. At the end of August 1938, Tolkien wrote to C. A. Furth at Allen & Unwin's an encouraging if also somewhat cryptic note, and for the first time gave the sequel a name *The Lord of the Ring*, not yet with an "s":

> In the last two or three days, after the benefit of idleness and open air, and the sanctioned neglect of duty, I have begun again on the sequel to the "Hobbit"—*The Lord of the Ring*. It is now flowing along and getting quite out of hand. It has reached about Chapter VII and progresses toward quite unforeseen goals. I must say I think it is a good deal better in places and some ways than the predecessor; but that does not say that I think it either more suitable or more adapted for its audience. For one thing it is, like my own children (who have the immediate serial rights), rather "older"....
> If the weather is wet in the next fortnight we may have got still further on. But it is no bed-time story.
>
> (Carpenter, ed., *Letters:* 40–1)

About a month and a half later, in a letter to Stanley Unwin, Tolkien made himself clearer:

> When I spoke, in an earlier letter to Mr. Furth, of this sequel getting "out of hand", I did not mean it to be complimentary to the process. I really only meant it was ... becoming more terrifying than the Hobbit. It may prove quite unsuitable. It is more "adult".... The darkness of the present days has had some effect on it.
>
> (Carpenter, ed., *Letters:* 41)

Elements like the black riders who pursue the hobbits were entering into his work. The spirit of the time was entering the work, too. No longer is the motive a hobbit setting out on an adventure. Now a dangerous force threatens and a hobbit is driven from his comfortable home on a heroic mission. It was October 1938; Hitler had begun his rampage for universal power; Europe was on the brink of war. Little people everywhere were in peril.

A reader, consequently, could see reflected in *The Lord of the Rings* (a mythical story set in a mythical landscape during a mythical time cycle) the events of the European catastrophe of the mid-nineteen-hundreds. There is a common theme to both "stories:" the exercise of power is evil and it also threatens to corrupt those whom it endangers and who are called upon, and undertake, to oppose it. If "power" in the last sentence were written with a capital "P," and personified, The *Lord of the Rings* could be categorized as an allegory. But that would offend Tolkien greatly:

> As for any inner meaning or 'message', it [*The Lord of the Rings*] has in the intention of the author none. It is neither allegorical nor topical…. I cordially dislike allegory in all its manifestations, and always have done so since I grew old and wary enough to detect its presence. I much prefer history, true or feigned, with its varied applicability to the thought and experience of readers. I think that many confuse "applicability" with "allegory"; but the one resides in the freedom of the reader, and the other in the purposed domination of the author.
>
> (*Fellowship:* 6–7)

The book is *about* power, among other things. But "Power," is not a character, under that name or another, embodied in the story as figures are in certain medieval works like the *Romance of the Rose* or *The Castle of Perseverance*. The characteristic which gives myth meaning, Tolkien believed, was not allegory but applicability. Myth does not represent a particular something but can be applied to many situations. The story he wrote, Tolkien believed, is one representation of God-given truth. That truth is presented in the form of a particular story, a myth, which is applicable to other stories or situations and shows their essential frame or skeleton or pattern.

Tolkien worked on *The Lord of the Rings*—with several periods of interruption—from 1937 until 1954, when the first and second volumes, *The Fellowship of the Ring* and *The Two Towers* were published. He remained Rawlinson and Bosworth Professor of Anglo-Saxon at Oxford until 1945, when he was elected Merton Professor of English. It entailed a move from Exeter to Merton College, which he was pleased to make. He retained that post until his retirement in 1959. In a list of complaints at the end of 1939 about how his time was taken up he includes "the virtual headship of a department in this bewildered university." [letters. 44] Oxford was on a war footing. Men who had run various departments or served in assistant capacities had been made into soldiers. Tolkien lamented, "I have lost both my chief assistant and his understudy." (Carpenter, ed., *Letters*: 44) A year earlier, he excused his slow response to a letter by alluding to "our little local strife." (Carpenter, ed., *Letters*: 36) When the position of Professor of Poetry at Oxford became vacant, Tolkien and C.S. Lewis joined forces to secure, successfully, the election of the Rev. Adam Fox, opposing two other more favored, and more liberal candidates. As part of his duties, too, Tolkien continued to write scholarly articles on philological subjects, like "MS Bodley 34: A re-collation of a collation", which appeared in *Studia Neophilologica* in 1947. He also wrote the preface for the 1940 Allen & Unwin edition of Charles Wrenn's revision of John R. Clark Hall's modern English translation of *Beowulf* and of the *Finnesburg Fragment*. Tolkien was slow to write the preface and lax in responding to inquiries from his publisher. Tolkien's courtly reply to Stanley Unwin's anxious letter about when he would get the promised but undelivered preface gives a good picture of what life was like for Tolkien during those years:

> Apologies would be vain in the face of my vexatious and uncivil behavior…. [M]any disasters have befallen me…. (It may mitigate your just wrath if I say that since I wrote in December my wife's health became much worse. I spent most of last term in an attic in

a hotel, with my house derelict and damaged. [The water pipes burst in his house during the winter of 1939–1940.] I have been ill myself, and hardly able to cope with university work, which for me has trebled.)

(Carpenter, ed., Letters: 45)

Health, indeed, was a continuing problem in the Tolkien family. In a number of letters Tolkien makes passing reference to illness, accident, and indisposition. In 1939, for example, at the beginning of the year, Tolkien had a case of influenza, which "has not damaged me much, though it caught me in a state of exam-exhaustion; but my throat seems to be getting worse, and I don't feel bright." (Carpenter, ed., *Letters*: 43) During the summer, he injured himself while gardening and the "accident ... left me very unwell for a long while." At the same time there was "the further blow of my wife's illness," (Carpenter, ed., *Letters*: 44) which lingered throughout summer and autumn and which was first feared to be cancer, although it turned out not to be. Edith's ill-health is a recurring misfortune. In 1958, for example, Tolkien reports that she was ill nearly the entire year and, with painful irony that she "celebrated the return of health by a fall in the garden, smashing up her left arm so badly that she is ... crippled and in plaster." (Carpenter, ed., *Letters*: 296) In July 1962, he wrote to his Aunt Jane about his lumbago and Edith's double affliction, arthritis and painful "internal lesions." In 1968, Tolkien himself was in hospital because of a fall, and the next year his doctor was very concerned about his gall bladder. Christopher's health, too, was for a while of serious concern to his parents. During 1938, he was "confined to bed with irregularities of the heart ... which caused him to be a total invalid for several years. (Carpenter, ed., *Letters*: 435) Michael had enlisted in the army, at the beginning of the war with Hitler. Late in 1940 or early in 1941, he was injured in a training accident and sent to a hospital in Worcester. (Carpenter, ed., *Letters*: 47)

Illnesses, the children's education and just the routine upkeep of his family made a serious financial burden for Tolkien. Prestigious as being a Professor at Oxford was, it was not well-paid. For years, Tolkien took summer work marking State Certificate exam papers, which he detested. Even after the publication of *The Hobbit*, money matters were not easy. In the letter to his Aunt Jane, in which he spoke of Edith's arthritis, responding to his aunt's offer to return a gift check he had sent her so that he can put the money into a wheel chair for Edith, Tolkien discussed the vicissitudes of his financial situation, demonstrated the generosity of his character and reiterated his frustration at the British tax system:

> Only a little while ago I was wondering if we should be able to go on living here, on my inadequate pension, of which I feel it proper to give away at least what the Tax collectors leave in my hands (a National one: I refused the University pension, and took the lump sum and invested it in a trust managed by my bank). All this, simply to assure you that the little gift was a personal pleasure, hardly worth much thanks; also to assure you that I can help more if needed.
>
> (Carpenter, ed., *Letters:* 315–6)

Even in 1965, when his books were already selling quite well but had not yet become a phenomenon, he expressed anxiety over money and complained about the severity of taxation:

> I think it unlikely that we shall move from Oxford. Anywhere in sight of the sea proves vastly expensive…. I am not "rolling in gold", but by continuing to work I am (so far) continuing to have an income about the same as a professor-in-cathedra, which leaves me a margin above my needs nowadays.
>
> (Carpenter, ed., *Letters:* 363–4)

Tolkien's growing fame once *The Hobbit* was published seems not really to have effected his career at Oxford. He was still overworked, underpaid, highly esteemed and one of a group of influential and convivial scholars and writers. Part of Tolkien's fame at Oxford rested surprisingly on the quality of his dramatic recitation. Although he was notorious for the inaudibility, rapidity and mumbled character of his speech, when he recited Beowulf or Chaucer, he was according to many, including W.H. Auden, who had attended his classes as an undergraduate, astonishing and riveting. In the summer of 1938, John Masefield, the Poet Laureate of England at the time, and Tolkien's colleague, Neville Coghill, organized *Summer Diversions*, a series of academic entertainments at Oxford. Tolkien appeared as Chaucer and recited the *Nun's Priest's Tale* (the great barnyard story of the rooster Chauntecleer) from *The Canterbury Tales*.

Tolkien also performed in his academic role outside the immediate setting of Oxford. He lectured on dragons to children at the University Museum in January of 1938, and, the same month gave a lecture on BBC radio on Anglo-Saxon. Throughout his career he did radio broadcasts for the BBC. In 1953, for example, he introduced and spoke after a dramatized presentation of his translation of *Sir Gawain and the Green Knight.* (Carpenter, *Tolkien*: 141)

CHAPTER EIGHT

War, Politics, and Religion

Kilby then related an anecdote he had heard which involved [Tolkien's] attendance at mass not long after Vatican II. An expert in Latin, [Tolkien] had reluctantly composed himself to its abolishment in favor of English. But when he arrived next time at services and seated himself in the middle of a bench, he began to notice other changes than the language, one a diminution of genuflection. His disappointment was such that he rose up and made his way awkwardly to the aisle and there made three very low bows, then stomped out of the church.

(Birzer, 49)

TOLKIEN REMAINED IN OXFORD during the Second World War. His life was different from what it had been, however. He was busier, and he suffered the same privations and burdens as all other English people, shortages, lines, blackouts, closed pubs, war-related duties. In addition, during the blitz in 1942, the entire back stock of *The Hobbit* was destroyed. Tolkien had already seen the projected publication of a German version of *The Hobbit* scuttled.

In the summer of 1938, he received a letter from the German publishing company which was planning to issue his book in Germany checking on his "arisch" [aryan] origin. He wrote to Stanley Unwin:

> Personally, I should be inclined to refuse to give any Bestätigung [confirmation] (although it happens I can) and let the German translation go hang.... I should object strongly to any such declaration appearing in print. I do not regard the probable absence of all Jewish blood as necessarily honourable ... and should regret giving any colour to the notion that I subscribed to the wholly pernicious and unscientific race doctrines.
>
> (Carpenter, ed., *Letters:* 37)

However, since it appeared to Tolkien that Allen & Unwin had a serious financial stake in the matter, he felt under obligation to the firm's interest as well as to his own principles. He wrote, therefore, two drafts of a response, one, a refusal even to supply such information, the other, should Allen & Unwin wish to use it, a polite but unyielding reply to the German publishers, mobilizing a little bit of philology against them:

> ...I regret that I am not clear as to what you intend by arisch. I am not of Aryan extraction: that is Indo-iranian; as far as I am aware none of my ancestors spoke Hindustani, Persian, Gypsy, or any related dialects. But if I am to understand that you are enquiring whether I am of *Jewish* origin, I can only reply that I regret that I appear to have no ancestors of that gifted people.
>
> (Carpenter, ed., *Letters:* 37)

His publishers sent the flat refusal. "I suppose," Tolkien wrote to Stanley Unwin on December 19, 1939, "the German edition of *The Hobbit* will probably never appear now." (Carpenter, ed., *Letters:* 44) The first German translation of *The Hobbit* appeared in 1957.

His letters to Christopher show him dealing with bicycle tire punctures and standing on queues to buy "one slab of pork-pie," of mowing lawns and helping to grow food, and even of building chicken coops and taking care of chickens:

> 3:45 Wed.... Arrived back to find Biddy [a hen] had broken another egg (about the 7th), so ... I have spent an agreeable time catching her (i.e., the bird), cleaning her, trimming her and disinfecting her—and then disinfecting myself. Grr! The fourth lawn will have to wait.
>
> (Carpenter, ed., *Letters:* 74)

In a letter dated the third of April, 1944, which he sent to Christopher, Tolkien gives a telling portrait of himself and of the wartime ambience around Oxford as he relates a conversation he had with a young American officer:

> I did ... get a dim notion into his head that the "Oxford Accent" (by which he politely told me he meant mine) was not "forced" and "put on", but a natural one.... After I told him that his "accent" sounded to me like English after being wiped over with a dirty sponge, and suggested (falsely) to an English observer that, together with American slouch, it indicated a slovenly and ill-disciplined people—well, we got quite friendly. We had some bad coffee in the refreshment room at Snow Hill, and parted.
>
> (Carpenter, ed., *Letters:* 69–70)

On Fridays, Tolkien served as an air raid warden and slept at the area headquarters. (Carpenter, ed., *Letters:* 63) In one letter, he writes that he "sat up 'on duty, till 1:30 this morn." (Carpenter, ed., *Letters:* 74) In another he describes this duty more fully: "Then I had to go and sleep (???) at C[ompany] HeadQ[uarters]. I did not—not much. I was in the small C33 room: very cold and damp." He had also been tapped by the government to be a cryptographer for the British foreign office. After being trained, he was never called.

At the university, too, he had a great amount more work than before the war. In addition two of his sons were fighting in the war. Michael was in the army and suffered physical and emotional injury, and was hospitalized. Christopher was in the RAF and was sent to Bloemfontein in South Africa, the place of Tolkien's birth. John had been studying for the priesthood in Italy at a seminary.

The war forced him to return to England. He continued his studies for the priesthood in Lancashire. Tolkien's wartime letters to Christopher afford not only a wealth of information about how Tolkien thought about *The Lord of the Rings*, but also the depth and strength of his attachment to Christopher.

Tolkien's attitudes towards the Second World War, Germany, German culture, and the German people were more complex and nuanced than wartime propaganda demanded:

> People in this land seem not even yet to realize that in the Germans we have enemies whose virtues (and they are virtues) of obedience and patriotism are greater than ours in the mass. Whose brave men are just as brave as ours. Whose industry is about 10 times greater.
>
> (Carpenter, ed., *Letters:* 55)

But, he despised Hitler, continuing to say that the Germans, "under a curse of God," were "now led by a man inspired by a mad, whirlwind devil: a typhoon, a passion," who made "the poor old Kaiser [Wilhem, from the First World War] look like an old woman knitting." (Carpenter, ed., *Letters:* 55) Writing more fully he said:

> Anyway, I have in this War a burning private grudge—which would probably make me a better soldier at 49 than I was at 22: against that ruddy little ignoramus Adolf Hitler.... Ruining, perverting, misapplying, and making for ever accursed, that noble northern spirit, a supreme contribution to Europe, which I have ever loved, and tried to present in its true light.
>
> (Carpenter, ed., *Letters:* 55–6)

He did not see Hitler or Germany as the only evil. After the Teheran Conference in 1943, in which Roosevelt, Churchill and Stalin discussed military strategy against Germany and, tentatively, terms for a peace settlement, Tolkien wrote to Christopher about his concerns for the peace process. He expressed disbelief that the "bloodthirsty old murderer Josef Stalin could advocate the "aboli-

tion of tyrranny & intolerance." He was concerned about the out-
come of the war:

> I am not really sure that its victory is going to be so much better
> for the world as a whole and in the long run than the victory of —
> ——. I don't suppose letters in are censored. But if they are, or
> not, I need to you hardly add that them's the sentiments of a good
> many folk—and no indication of a lack of patriotism. For I love
> England (not Great Britain and certainly not the British Common-
> wealth (grr!)), and if I was of military age, I should, I fancy, be
> grousing away in a fighting service, and willing to go on to the
> bitter end—always hoping that things may turn out better for
> England than they look like doing. (Carpenter, ed., *Letters*: 65)

The dash, of course, replaces "Germany." The complexity of his
position results from the broadness of his perspective. It is a perspective that gave him divided loyalties, not in the sense of an
ambivalence in his support for an Allied victory over the Axis
powers. His loyalty was divided between an overriding loyalty to
what he saw as eternal Divine truth and the best one can do in the
fallen temporal world. His eternal perspective tempered his vision
of the world. As a Roman Catholic he believed this a fallen world,
that error and woe are not only inescapable but the very nature of
existence. In 1944 he wrote to Christopher:

> We knew Hitler was a vulgar and ignorant little cad, in addition to
> any other defects (or the source of them) but there seem to be
> many v[ulgar] and i[gnorant] cads who don't speak German, and
> who given the same chance would show most of the other Hit-
> lerian characteristics.
>
> (Carpenter, ed., *Letters:* 93)

The duality of Tolkien's vision is just as strong in his attitude
toward war itself. In the letters to Christopher excerpted above, he
frequently states that, were he of age, he would be fighting in the
war against the Germans, too. Nevertheless, when he wrote of war,
he condemned it outright before he accepted it:

The utter stupid waste of war, not only material but moral and spiritual, is so staggering to those who have to endure it. And always was (despite the poets) and always will be (despite the propagandists)—not of course that it has not [been,] is and will be necessary to face it in an evil world.

(Carpenter, ed., *Letters:* 75)

Similarly, after the American atomic bombing of Japan Tolkien wrote to Christopher on August 9, 1945:

The news about "Atomic bombs" is so horrifying one is stunned. The utter folly of these lunatic physicists to consent to do such work for war purposes: calmly plotting the destruction of the world! Such explosives in men's hands, while their moral and intellectual status is declining, is about as useful as giving out firearms to all inmates of a gaol and then saying that you hope "this will insure peace". But one good thing may arise out of it, I suppose, if the write-ups are not overheated. Japan ought to cave in. Well, we're in God's hands. But he does not look kindly on Babel-builders.

(Carpenter, ed., *Letters:* 116)

Tolkien saw all of the participants in the war as collaborators in evil because, using imagery from *The Lord of the Rings,* "we are attempting to conquer Sauron with the Ring.... But the penalty is ... to breed new Saurons, and slowly turn Men into Elves and Orcs.... and we started out with many Orcs on our side." (Carpenter, ed. *Letters:* 78)

In the Forward to *The Lord of the Rings* Tolkien describes the Second World War by showing how the war in *The Lord of the Ring* is *not* like it:

The real war does not resemble the legendary war in its process or its conclusion. If it had inspired or directed the development of the legend, then certainly the Ring would have been seized and used against Sauron; he would not have been destroyed but occupied.

(*Fellowship:* 6)

In other words, Tolkien sees using power against power as establishing the rule of power, for Tolkien a negative no matter who wields power because of the fallen nature of mankind. For the same reason, that mankind is fallen, Tolkien can say that he does not favor democracy.

Politically, Tolkien called himself a "reactionary back number." (Carpenter, ed., *Letters*: 65) He was not happy with progress and mechanization nor with centering an understanding of life on matter at the expense of spirit. (Carpenter, ed., *Letters*: 110) His distaste for modernization and what he saw as its pernicious effects can be seen clearly in the letter he wrote to Christopher describing his train trip with the New Englander. He writes of his time spent in Birmingham, his destination, where he had grown up and gone to King Edward's:

> I then strolled about my "home town" for a bit. Except for one patch of ghastly wreckage (opp[osite] my old school's site) it does not look much damaged: not by the enemy. The chief damage has been the growth of great flat featureless modern buildings.
>
> (Carpenter, ed., *Letters:* 70)

Writing to Christopher in 1943, he defined his politics in a very unsystematic and even impulsive way, not the least deterred by internal contradictions. He began:

> My political opinions lean more and more to Anarchy (philosophically understood, meaning abolition of control not whiskered men with bombs) —or to "unconstitutional" Monarchy.

He proceeded with more bluster than intent:

> I would arrest anybody who uses the word State (in any sense other than the inanimate realm of England and its inhabitants, a thing that has neither power, rights nor mind); and after a chance of recantation, execute them if they remained obstinate! Government is an abstract noun meaning the art and process of governing and it should be an offence to write it with a capital G or as to refer to people.

Despite this fantasy of power—he has imagined himself to be the person of the Government—he continued:

> the most improper job of any man, even saints (who at any rate were at least unwilling to take it on), is bossing other men. Not one in a million is fit for it, and least of all those who seek the opportunity.

By the end of the letter which began with a distinction between philosophical anarchism and bomb throwers, Tolkien has forgotten that distinction, or it is no longer useful for expressing his feeling:

> There is only one bright spot and that is the growing habit of disgruntled men of dynamiting factories and power stations.... But it won't do any good, if it is not universal.
>
> (Carpenter, ed., *Letters:* 63–4)

He is expressing his rage at the course of social development, not setting forth a real program to which he is dedicated. His true heart's belief by which his actions were guided is expressed not by these sentiments but by his sense "that Our Lord actually is more pained by offences we commit against one another than those we commit against himself." (Carpenter, ed., *Letters:* 97) Tolkien's real dedication is to his religious faith, as he makes clear in the letter's final paragraph:

> We were born in a dark age out of due time.... But there is this comfort: otherwise we should not know, or so much love, what we do love. I imagine the fish out of water is the only fish to have an inkling of water.
>
> (Carpenter, ed., *Letters:* 64)

The experience of the wretchedness of the fallen world is what makes clear what the nature of the unfallen world is like. The connection between Tolkien's politics and his Faith is fundamental. "I am not a 'democrat,'" Tolkien declared,

if only because "humility" and equality are spiritual principles cor-
rupted by the attempt to mechanize and formalize them, with the
result that we get not universal smallness and humility, but universal greatness and pride.

(Carpenter, 192)

His support for the Roman Catholic Church, in fact, colored his
political sympathies. His antipathy to communism, for
example,—he ranked Stalin as more evil than Hitler—was in large
part because of its atheist ideology and the reports he heard from
the poet Roy Campbell, who had fought on the fascist side during
the Spanish Civil War, that the communists in Spain murdered
Roman Catholic priests. (Carpenter, 192) Because General Franco
supported the Church, Tolkien, not a supporter of fascism, gave
his sympathies to fascism in Spain.

Tolkien was primarily a man of feeling and sensation; his
thoughts and ideas were founded upon or responses to deep and
strong feeling, though incorporating such elements as fact, myth,
reason, and imagination. As a philologist, for example, he got "a
large part of ... aesthetic pleasure ... from the *form* of words (and
especially from the *fresh* association of word-form with word-
sense)." (Carpenter, ed., *Letters*: 172) He was grounded in his
Roman Catholicism, an all important and unifying force in his
life, his salvation, not by thought but by the deepest and tenderest
bond of child to mother, and in his case made even stronger
because it was orphan child to lost mother. When Tolkien wrote of
the strengths of Roman Catholicism he referred to its sensual artifacts: "The only cure for sagging of fainting faith is Communion,"
he wrote to Michael when Michael was suffering a crisis of faith.
Later in the same letter, he attributes his constancy in faith to the
fact that "I fell in love with the blessed sacrament." (Carpenter,
ed., *Letters*: 338, 340)

Tolkien's politics had a half-life he did not intend and was not
entirely happy with. Many in the several movements of the 1960s
found his anti-mechanical attitudes and his disdain for the industrial revolution congenial. They found solace and sustenance in his
love of myth and fantasy and in his stark vision of the conflict

between essentially good simple folk and the evil and imperial design of those with power or who lusted after it. It was, in part, this very conservatism which made Tolkien particularly attractive to many of the radical young. No matter what the political label, they shared his feelings and enjoyed escape through imagination, and would have no trouble agreeing with Tolkien that escape was a good thing. Those who condemn escape, Tolkien remarked, were those who wanted to keep people in prison. Tolkien, however, was not a utopian nor even really a reformer. He accepted war despite his conviction that it is absurd, and he believed in the inevitability of evil because he believed literally in the fact of the Fall of Man and, consequently, in this world as a fallen world. He also devoutly believed in the possibility, through the grace and sacrifice of the crucified Christ, of eternal salvation.

CHAPTER NINE

Culminations

Here are beauties which pierce like swords or burn like cold iron.

> —C.S. Lewis on the publication of
> *The Fellowship of the Ring.*

IN 1947, TOLKIEN SHOWED Rayner Unwin a nearly completed manuscript of *The Lord of the Rings*. Rayner was no longer the ten-year-old who had earned a shilling from his father, Tolkien's publisher, Stanley Unwin, for writing his opinion of *The Hobbit*. He was an undergraduate at Oxford. Tolkien had been showing him parts of the book since 1937 when he had begun writing it. This time Rayner wrote to his father that *The Lord of the Rings* is "a weird book.... Quite honestly I don't know who is expected to read it, but if grown ups will not feel infra dig to read it many will undoubtedly enjoy themselves." (Carpenter, *Tolkien*: 202)

In 1949, Tolkien gave the manuscript, now satisfied that it was complete, to C.S. Lewis. Like Rayner Unwin he had followed its progress throughout its composition. After reading the book in its entirety, he wrote to Tolkien:

> I have drained a rich cup and satisfied a long thirst. Once it really gets under weigh the steady upward slope of grandeur and terror

(not unrelieved by green dells, without which it would be intolerable) is almost unequalled in the whole range of narrative art known to me.... No romance can repel the charge of "escapism" with such confidence. If it errs, it errs in precisely the opposite direction: all victories of hope deferred and the piling up of odds against the heroes are near to being too painful.... I congratulate you. All the long years you have spent on it are justified.

(Carpenter, Tolkien: 204)

His labors, however, almost did not bear the fruit of publication because Tolkien was dissatisfied and angry with Allen & Unwin. He was eager to see not only the publication of *The Lord of the Rings*, but with it the publication of *The Silmarillion*. Tolkien had shown *The Silmarillion* to Allen and Unwin in 1937. At that time, the firm was looking for a sequel to *The Hobbit* and rejected it, not on its lack of merit, Stanley Unwin said, but because it did not fit the bill, and it was not complete or even in order. Tolkien also felt the firm had not properly publicized his book *Farmer Giles of Ham*, which they had published in 1949. When Stanley Unwin told Tolkien that *Farmer Giles* "had only sold 2000 copies," and that it had "not yet done as well as we had hoped," Tolkien wrote back, "I have observed no advertisements." (Carpenter, ed., *Letters:* 138, 140) Consequently, he was brusquely aggressive in negotiations with the firm, especially because Gervase Mathew, a Dominican priest and a scholar who frequently attended meetings of the *Inklings*, had introduced him to Milton Waldman of the publishing firm Collins, and Tolkien hoped to be able to offer both books to Collins.

Waldman told Tolkien that Collins would be interested in publishing the sequel to *The Hobbit*. Tolkien then sent him not *The Lord of the Rings* but *The Silmarillion*. After Waldman told Tolkien that Collins would publish *The Silmarillion* if he finished it, only then Tolkien gave him *The Lord of the Rings* to read. Waldman wanted to publish it and wrote to Tolkien asking whether he was free to offer it to Collins or if he had any legal or moral commitment to Allen & Unwin. Tolkien responded:

I believe myself to have no *legal* obligation to Allen and Unwin, since the clause in The Hobbit contract with regard to offering the next book seems to have been satisfied either a) by their rejection of *The Silmarillion* or b) by their eventual acceptance and publication of Farmer Giles. I should (as you note) be glad to leave them, as I have found them in various ways unsatisfactory.

(Carpenter, ed., *Letters*: 135)

There followed a series of polite but unhappy letters between Tolkien and Stanley Unwin in which Tolkien strove to free himself from what he took to be the serpentine coils of his publisher. To that end, he went on at great length arguing how limited the appeal of *The Lord of the Rings* would be. Tolkien was offended that Stanley Unwin had proposed that *The Lord of the Rings* and *The Silmarillion* be published in a number of volumes after both manuscripts had been cut. He was bitter, too, about the past rejection of *The Silmarillion*. And he was infuriated by Rayner's letter from the United States, where he was studying at Harvard, to his father, not intended for Tolkien's eyes, which Sir Stanley nevertheless had sent him, in which Rayner wrote:

The Lord of the Rings is a very great book in its own curious way and deserves to be produced somehow. I never felt the lack of a *Silmarillion* when reading it. But although he claims not to contemplate any drastic rewriting ... surely this is a case for an editor who would incorporate any really relevant material from *The Silmarillion* into *The Lord of the Rings* without increasing the already enormous bulk of the latter and, if feasible, even cutting it. Tolkien wouldn't do it, but someone whom he would trust and who had sympathy (one of his sons?) might possibly do it. If this is not workable I would say publish *The Lord of the Rings* as a prestige book, and after having a second look at it, drop *The Silmarillion*.

(Carpenter, ed., *Letters:* 140)

Tolkien wrote back to Stanley Unwin that

the question of "dropping" *The Silmarillion,* after a discrete feint, and taking *The Lord* (edited) just does not arise. I have not offered, am not offering *The Lord of the Rings* to you, or to anyone else, on such conditions—as surely I made plain before. I want a decision, yes or no: to the proposal I made: and not to any imagined possibility.

Stanley Unwin took the challenge and responded with a "no," expressing his sorrow at being presented with an ultimatum and adding that "it might well have been yes given time and the sight of the typescript." (Carpenter, *Tolkien:* 210)

Tolkien was honest in his anger, yet it also served his purpose, and he was freed from obligations to Allen & Unwin and could go with Collins in good conscience. But Collins was no more forthcoming than Allen & Unwin. Essentially the same drama that Tolkien had played out at Allen & Unwin was repeated with Waldman and William Collins. Tolkien gave William Collins the same ultimatum he had given Stanley Unwin, except that now it was only with regard to *The Lord of the Rings* since *The Silmarillion* was not yet ready for publication even if a publisher had been immediately prepared to publish it. William Collins' reply was the same as Stanley Unwin's. It was now 1952 and Tolkien hadn't a publisher for either of the works he so cherished. Bad experience, however, had mellowed him and a kind letter from Rayner Unwin, who must have known what was going on in publishing circles, asking about the publication plans for *The Lord of the Rings* and *The Silmarillion* melted his resentment. He responded to Rayner Unwin on June 22, 1952 in a letter marked by the amount of personal material in it and giving the picture of a man overburdened with labor and a sense of loss who was grateful for Rayner's generous spirit: "How kind of you to write again! I have behaved badly," he wrote

(...) As for *The Lord of the Rings* and *The Silmarillion*, they are where they were. The one finished (and the end revised), and the other still unfinished (or unrevised), and both gathering dust. I have been both off and on too unwell, and too burdened to do much about them, and too downhearted. ...But I have rather modified my views. Better something than nothing! Although to me all are one, and the "L of the Rings" would be better far (and eased) as part of the whole, I would gladly consider the publication of any part of this stuff.

(Carpenter, ed., *Letters:* 163)

Within a week Rayner Unwin wrote back "We do *want* to publish for you—it's only ways and means that have held us up." (Carpenter, ed., *Letters:* 163–4) Ways and means were difficult for Tolkien, too. He had only one manuscript copy of *The Lord of the Rings* which he had typed himself since the cost of a professional typist was prohibitive, and he did not want to send the book through the mail. At the end of August, he took a week away from Oxford and went to his son Michael's cottage in Berkshire, where Michael was a schoolmaster nearby, while Michael and his family were away on vacation, so that he could correct the manuscript. Shortly after Tolkien returned to Oxford around September 10th, Rayner Unwin visited him and picked up the manuscript. He knew the book well enough not to have to read it again and began immediately to check with several printers on costs, got a confirmation from his father, who was in Japan, and on November 10th of 1952 wrote to Tolkien that Allen & Unwin would like to publish the book uncut but divided into three volumes. Because it was a highly risky venture, in order to reduce the firm's anticipated losses, the publishing agreement between the firm and Tolkien would be that Tolkien would receive no royalties for the book. Once the cost of publishing the book had been recovered, Tolkien and Allen & Unwin would split the profits fifty-fifty, ultimately an extremely advantageous arrangement for Tolkien should the book succeed, which, of course, it did beyond any expectation.

Tolkien delivered the manuscript for publication in April 1953. Edith had suffered "increasing ill health" since November, and "on a doctor's ultimatum," Tolkien was "obliged to spend most of what time I could spare from duties in finding and negotiating for the purchase of a house on high dry soil in the quiet." The house they lived in on Holywell Street in Oxford had become unbearable because of the noise and the fumes from the greatly increased motor traffic. The move was particularly difficult because it made it hard for Tolkien to get to his files or to find anything because of their disarrangement. He was also "involved as chairman [of the English Department at Oxford] in controlling the setting of all the honours English papers for June." (Carpenter, ed., *Letters*: 166) And on the fifteenth of April he delivered the W. P. Ker Lecture at the University of Glasgow on the temptation to adultery in *Sir Gawain and the Green Knight.*

The first two volumes of *The Lord of the Rings—The Fellowship of the Ring* and *The Two Towers*—were published in 1954, and the last volume, *The Return of the King* was published in 1955. Allen & Unwin expected the book to sell modestly and printed three and a half thousand copies of *The Fellowship of the Ring.* Six weeks after publication, the stock had sold out and a reprint was necessary. Between 1954 and 1966, until the second edition of *The Lord of the Rings* was published, *The Fellowship* was reprinted in England fourteen times, *The Two Towers* eleven times and *The Return of the King*, ten times. In 1956, the first translation (into Dutch) of *The Lord of the Rings* appeared followed soon after by translations into Swedish, Polish, Danish, German, Italian, French, Japanese, Finnish, Norwegian, Hebrew, Hungarian, Icelandic, and Spanish. The book recouped printing and publishing expenses a year after the publication of *The Return of the King*, and early in 1956, Tolkien received his first "half-profits" check from Allen & Unwin for more than thirty-five hundred pounds, around $15,000 U.S. dollars, which was quite a bit more than his annual salary at Oxford. In 1957, he sold the manuscripts *of The Hobbit, The Lord of the Rings, Farmer Giles of Ham,* and *Mr. Bliss* to Marquette University, a Roman Catholic school in Milwaukee, Wisconsin, for twelve hundred and fifty pounds—about $5000 U.S. dollars.

Critical response to *The Lord of the Rings* was divided. W. H. Auden, who had written in a review of the book in *The New York Times* that "[n]o fiction I have read in the last five years has given me more joy," (Carpenter, *Tolkien*: 221) accurately characterized the critical reaction this way: "Nobody seems to have a moderate opinion; either, like myself, people find it a masterpiece of its genre, or they cannot abide it." (Carpenter, *Tolkien:* 223) Tolkien summed it up in verse:

> The Lord of the Rings
> is one of those things:
> if you like it you do:
> if you don't, then you boo!
>
> (Carpenter, *Tolkien:* 223)

C. S. Lewis was, again, one of those who liked it very much, and he wrote in the August 14, 1954 issue of *Time & Tide:*

> This book is like lightening from a clear sky. To say that in it heroic romance, gorgeous, eloquent, and unashamed, has suddenly returned at a period almost pathological in its anti-romanticism, is inadequate.... [I]n the history of Romance—a history which stretches back to the Odyssey and beyond—it makes not a return but an advance or revolution: the conquest of new territory.
>
> (Carpenter, *Tolkien:* 219)

The reviewer in the September 18, 1954 issue of *The New Statesman,* Naomi Mitchison, wrote that *The Lord of the Rings* was "extraordinary, terrifying and beautiful." A.E. Cherryman wrote in the August 6, 1954 issue of *Truth,* "It is an amazing piece of work.... [Tolkien] has added something, not only to the world's literature, but to its history." The reviewer in the August 13, 1954 issue of the *Oxford Times* called the book "extraordinary and often beautiful." Howard Spring wrote in the August 26th issue of *Country Life:* "This is a work of art.... It has invention, fancy and imagination.... It is a profound parable of man's everlasting struggle against evil."

The negative reviews, too, often granted something to Tolkien. Peter Green, biographer of Kenneth Grahame, author of the classic, *The Wind in the Willows,* wrote in the August 27th edition of the Daily Telegraph, "I presume [*The Fellowship of the Ring*] is meant to be taken seriously, and am apprehensive that I can find no really adequate reason for doing so.... And yet this shapeless work has an undeniable fascination." Even Edwin Muir, who was much less enthusiastic about Tolkien's work, in a review of *The Two Towers* in the November 21, 1954 issue of the *Observer* had some praise. Of the ents, he wrote: "Symbolically they are quite convincing, yet they are full of character, too, as formidable and strange as a forest of trees going to war." But Muir sounded the keynote for negative criticism when he wrote:

> The astonishing thing is that all the characters are boys mas-
> querading as adult heroes. The hobbits, or halflings, are ordinary
> boys; the fully human heroes have reached the fifth form; but
> hardly one of them knows anything about women, except by
> hearsay. Even the elves and the dwarfs and the ents are boys, irre-
> trievably, and will never come to puberty.
>
> (Carpenter, *Tolkien:* 223)

Maurice Richardson, writing in the December 18, 1954 issue of *The New Statesman* voiced the same objection: "It is all I can do to restrain myself from shouting.... 'Adults of all ages! Unite against the infantilist invasion.'"

Perhaps Tolkien's severest critic was Edmund Wilson in *The Nation*. Not only did he criticize Tolkien, but Tolkien's admirers, too. Wilson began by asking,

> why [Tolkien] should have supposed he was writing for adults.
> There are ... some details that are a little unpleasant for a chil-
> dren's book.... An overgrown fairy story, a philological
> curiosity—that is, then, what *The Lord of the Rings* really is. The
> pretentiousness is all on the part of Dr. Tolkien's infatuated
> admirers.
>
> (Becker, 51)

At the same time that Tolkien's success as an author was beginning, recognition as a scholar was coming to him. In 1954, he
traveled to Dublin where he was awarded an honorary degree from
University College and to Belgium, where he received an honorary
degree from the University of Liège. He was elected Vice President

of the Philological society of Great Britain. He was unable, because of Edith's bad health, to travel to the United States to receive honorary degrees from Marquette and Harvard. When he retired from Oxford in 1959 he was awarded honorary fellowships by both Merton and Exeter Colleges. His children, too, had each achieved a place in the world. John was the Roman Catholic priest at Keele University, Michael the headmaster of a Benedictine school in Yorkshire, Christopher was a fellow at Oxford and soon, like his father teaching Anglo-Saxon there, and Priscilla became a teacher and a social worker. Michael and Christopher both married and Tolkien became a grandfather. Tolkien's bond with Christopher was particularly strong especially as Christopher became a partner in his work and expositor of his mythology. Christopher drew maps for his stories and entered into the details of the entire Tolkien-created mythology with as much energy and familiarity as his father. "I am," he told William Cater around 1976, speaking of J.R.R. Tolkien:

> the person most likely to know what he was about. And the knowledge that he wanted me to be his literary executor gave me the confidence to do it. I could not help him in his lifetime as much as I wished, for just to sort out his papers, which were in an enormous mess, would have meant asking him to step aside from them for a year or two. Since his death I've seen far more of his total literary and moral purpose than before. I've had his whole opus spread out in front of me, letters, papers, essays—and more than he ever had, because of the confusion the papers were in.
>
> (Becker, 93–4)

By the mid nineteen-sixties, it was evident that Tolkien had not only become successful but that he had become a phenomenon whose work had entered into the popular imagination. Successful as it was, *The Lord of the Rings* was only gathering momentum while it remained in hardback, but with the printing of the first paperback edition in 1965, it became a mass phenomenon spreading among students the way J.D. Salinger's *The Catcher in the Rye* or William Golding's *The Lord of the Flies* had. Ironically the company which was responsible for the popular explosion of Tolkien's epic was also engaged in denying to him the fruits of it.

In 1965, Ace, an American science-fiction paperback book publisher, decided to put out a paperback edition of *The Lord of the Rings*. At the time, U.S. copyright laws were lax enough to make such a move possible. Tolkien's American publisher, Houghton Mifflin, realized the necessity of marketing a paperback edition of its own and contracted to do so with Ballantine Books. In order to secure the copyright, however, the new edition had to be a revised edition, which Ballantine wanted to get out before the Ace edition. Rayner Unwin contacted Tolkien, apprised him that a pirate edition of *The Lord of the Rings* was about to appear, and asked him to make revisions in *The Lord of the Rings* and in *The Hobbit* in order to protect his and the firm's ownership. Tolkien was engaged in several other projects at the time. He was revising *Smith of Wootton Major*, a new story, he was working on his translation of *Sir Gawain and the Green Knight*, and he was making notes on his poem in Elvish, *Namárië*, which the composer Donald Swann was setting to music as part of a Tolkien song-cycle. He also was often slow at getting to work. Before, therefore, Tolkien got the manuscript to Houghton Mifflin, Ace's edition was in the bookstores and selling. The Ballantine paperback, when it did appear was more expensive than the Ace. It paid royalties to the author; the pirated edition did not. Moreover the cover art for the pirated edition was actually superior and more in the spirit of the book than the garish cover of the authorized version. Thus the Ace edition was outselling the authorized one until Tolkien himself intervened. He had, since the publication of *The Lord of the Rings* been flooded with "fan mail" from readers, which he answered personally and often at length. He began to insert in each response a note "to the effect that the paperback edition of Ace Books is piratical and issued without the consent of my publishers or myself and of course without remuneration to us." (Carpenter, ed., *Letters*: 356) Tolkien's strategy was effective. It galvanized American enthusiasts to form a Tolkien Society and they set about persuading bookstore owners not to stock the Ace edition. The Ballantine edition, when it appeared, carried a notice from Tolkien reading "This paperback edition and no other has been published with my consent and cooperation. Those who approve of courtesy (at least) to living authors will purchase it and no other." Further pressure was directly exerted on Ace by the Science-Fiction Writers of America. Ace capitulated, contacted Tolkien, paid him royalties on the books which had been sold and promised not to reprint *The Lord of the Rings* when the stock ran out. The effect of the pirate edition, ultimately, rather than proving injurious to Tolkien proved greatly beneficial in terms of publicity and sales.

Tolkien's popularity soared, especially among college students. He became inundated with fan mail, pictures, trinkets and requests. It was so overwhelming that Allen & Unwin dispatched a secretary to his home in Oxford once a week to help him deal with his mail. Worse than the mail were unexpected, uninvited guests showing up at his door wanting autographs or taking photographs or just wanting to meet him and talk about the world he had created. There were also telephone calls at all hours of the day and night from fans who hadn't stopped to think, for example, that when it is six in the evening in Los Angeles, it is two in the morning in England. Tolkien often voiced his displeasure to readers at becoming a cult figure, though he could not be entirely dismayed by it.

He did not, however, like his association with the psychedelic, "acid" culture, which took his books to be a sort of "trip." He wrote of many of his fans, "Art moves them and they don't know what they've been moved by and they get quite drunk on it. Many young Americans are involved in the stories in a way I'm not." (Carpenter, *Tolkien*: 231)

"I find it difficult to work—beginning to feel old and the fire dying down." Tolkien wrote that in his diary in 1965. On November 22, 1963, C.S. Lewis had died. Tolkien wrote to his daughter, Priscilla, four days after the death:

So far I have felt the normal feelings of a man of my age—like an old tree that is losing all its leaves one by one: this feels like an axe-blow near the roots. Very sad that we [Tolkien and Lewis] should

have been so separated in the last years; but our time of close communion endured in memory for both of us. I had a mass said this
morning, and was there, and served.

(Carpenter, ed., *Letters:* 341)

Nevertheless, Tolkien kept working. No longer teaching, he was
nevertheless engaged in correcting the proofs of his edition of *The
Ancrene Wisse*, revising his translations of *Gawain* and *Pearl,*
answering the many letters from readers fully, and revising his lecture on Fairy-Stories which Allen & Unwin wanted to reprint
paired in a volume with *Leaf by Niggle,* his story of a transit
through Purgatory. He also wrote *Smith of Wootton Major,* published in 1967, which he described as "an old man's story, filled
with the presage of bereavement," and which he explained was
"written with deep emotion, partly drawn from the experience of
the bereavement of "retirement" and of advancing age." (Carpenter, *Tolkien:* 243) All these projects kept him away from
bringing order and completion to *The Silmarillion.* When he did
have time, he often could not attend to *The Silmarillion* and spent
hours alone playing Patience (Solitaire) and drawing and still creating new words for his invented languages. Often, "the days seem
blank, and [he] cannot concentrate on anything. I find life such a
bore in this imprisonment." (Carpenter, *Tolkien:* 241) His retirement from Oxford removed Tolkien from the intellectual and
social stimulation he had enjoyed throughout his career. That, too,
no doubt accounted for his boredom and sense of bereavement.

But Tolkien's life was not an unrelieved gloom or even principally
gloomy, only that a sense of age and separation settled on him with
the heaviness and loneliness they can bring. He had visits from
friends and he and Edith had a weekly restaurant date with Norman
Davis and his wife. Davis had been a student of Tolkien's. In the
nineteen-sixties he was the Merton Professor of English Language
and Literature, formerly, Tolkien's professorship. Tolkien and Edith
celebrated their fiftieth wedding anniversary in 1966. As part of the
celebration, Donald Swann, composer, pianist and as one half of the
team of Flanders and Swann, performer, set a series of Tolkien's
poems to music as a song-cycle called, *The Road Goes Ever On.*

Other events like family visits and playing with grandchildren, who might stay with him and Edith a week at a time at the Miramar Hotel, also occupied them. Christopher's son, Simon, recalls:

> how incredibly nice he [Tolkien] was. His voice seemed deep, his laugh seemed full and his eyes seemed bright and full of life. He was always very elegantly dressed. I remember him taking off his jacket if we were going to play, and he'd always have a brightly coloured velvet waistcoat underneath. He was very conscious of the fact that my father had remarried and I was an only child, so he made a big fuss of me and we had a lot of fun. I had read *Lord of the Rings* at a very early age, and plagued him with endless questions about every small detail of it. He was incredibly patient. I never remember him being angry or upset in any way.
>
> (32)

Simon Tolkien's memories also reveal that despite Tolkien's strong religious convictions against divorce and remarriage, his disposition was gentle in such circumstances. Not only was he loving with his grandson, but his affection for Christopher and for Baillie, Christopher's second wife was not jeopardized.

Christopher's first wife, Faith, (Simon's mother) had made a plaster bust of Tolkien, which the English Faculty of Oxford wanted to be placed in the English Faculty Library. Tolkien had it "cast in bronze for the presentation." In writing of his appreciation of the honor to Norman Davis, Tolkien recalled the bust the Tsar of Russia had given to the library, which he (Tolkien) had often used to hang his hat on. (Carpenter, ed., *Letters*: 369) Tolkien was generous and charitable with the money he earned, and he and Edith lived well, but entirely without extravagance, essentially living the life they had always led but not having to scrimp. In Oxford, they lived in a small house, and Tolkien used the garage as his office. When they moved to Bournemouth to be by the sea, they lived in a cottage, and they often spent time at the nearby hotel, spending much of the day on the promenade, where Edith had many friends, too. On November 29, 1971, Edith died of an inflamed gall bladder. She was eighty-two.

After Edith died, Tolkien had no reason or desire to stay by the sea. He did not quite know where to go or how he wanted to live. At first, his old friend from King Edward's, C.L. Wiseman, the other surviving member of the T.C.B.S. "drew [him] from [his] lair in Bournemouth and took [him] to Milford." (Carpenter, ed., *Letters*: 429) In March he moved back to Oxford where he lived until his death. In a letter to his cousin Marjorie Incledon, with whom, as children, he had begun inventing languages, he explained how he got to Oxford:

> Owing to Christopher—when I was looking in vain for some-where to live he wrote "off his own bat" to the Warden of Merton College and said that his father was wandering looking in vain for a home, & could the College help? So I was amazed to receive a letter from the Warden saying that he had called a special meeting of the Governing Body, and it had unanimously voted that I should be invited to be a residential Fellow!
>
> (Carpenter, ed., *Letters:* 422)

During these last years he was not confined to Oxford, how-ever. He visited with Christopher and Baillie and their children, he went to Sidmouth with his daughter Priscilla and his grandson, Simon. He visited John at Stoke-on-Trent where he was parish priest, and John and Tolkien drove to Eyesham to spend time with Tolkien's brother Hilary on his fruit farm.

In his last years, too, Tolkien was the recipient of numerous honors. He turned down many invitations to the United States and honorary doctorates because he could not have endured the strain of travel. Oxford, however, conferred a Doctorate of Letters on him. And he went to Scotland to receive an honorary degree from the University of Edinburgh. On March 28, 1972, he was presented with a C.B.E. (Commander of the British Empire) by Queen Elizabeth II at Buckingham Palace. Afterwards, Rayner Unwin "held a dinner in his honour at the Garrick Club, and Allen & Unwin put him up at Brown's Hotel in London." (Carpenter, ed., *Letters*: 417) The depths of his affection for Rayner is reflected in the letter he wrote him after the event, in which he thanks Rayner for his kindness. It also gives a nice account of Tolkien's disposition during his last years:

> Inside the Palace the ceremonies were, especially for "recipients",
> accompanied by some tedium (with a few touches of the comic).
> But I was deeply moved by my brief meeting with the Queen, &
> our few words together. Quite unlike anything I had expected....
> Would it be possible for you to use my Christian name?... [A]s you
> are now a v. old friend, and a very dear one, I should much like
> also to be a "familiaris". R.
>
> (Carpenter, ed., *Letters:* 417–18)

Tolkien spent the last days of August 1973 first with friends in Cambridge and then in Bournemouth by the sea as a guest of Denis and Jocelyn Tolhurst. On the thirty-first of August, he was taken to a hospital in pain and diagnosed with an acute bleeding gastric ulcer. A chest infection then quickly developed. Michael was in Switzerland. Christopher was in France. They could not arrive at their father's bedside in time, but John and Priscilla were with Tolkien when he died Sunday morning, September 2, 1973. He was buried next to Edith in the Roman Catholic section of the cemetery at Wolvercote on the outskirts of Oxford.

Becker, Alida. *The Tolkien Scrapbook.* New York: Grosset & Dunlap, 1978, 192 p.

Birzer, Bradley J. *J.R.R. Tolkien's Sanctifying Myth: Understanding Middle-earth.* ISI Books, 2002, 219 p.

Carpenter, Humphrey. *The Inklings.* Boston: Houghton Mifflin, 1979, 287 p.

————. *Tolkien: A Biography.* Boston: Houghton Mifflin, 1977, 287 p.

————, ed. *The Letters of J.R.R. Tolkien.* With the assistance of Christopher Tolkien. Boston: Houghton Mifflin, 1981, 463 p.

Grotta-Kurska, Daniel. *J.R.R. Tolkien: Architect of Middle Earth: A Biography.* Edited by Frank Wilson. Philadelphia: Running Press, 1976, 165 p.

Helms, Randel. *Tolkien's World.* Boston: Houghton Mifflin, 1974, 167 p.

Lewis, C.S. *Surprised by Joy: The Shape of My Early Life.* New York: Harcourt, Brace & World, Inc., 1955, 238 p.

Rogers, Deborah Webster, and Ivor A. Rogers. *J.R.R. Tolkien.* Boston: Twayne Publishers, 1980, 164 p.

Tolkien, J.R.R. "On Fairy-Stories," in *Tree and Leaf.* Boston: The Riverside Press Cambridge, Houghton Mifflin, 1965.

————. *The Hobbit.* Boston: Houghton Mifflin, 1966.

————. *The Fellowship of the Ring.* Boston: Houghton Mifflin, 1965.

————. *The Father Christmas Letters.* Boston: Houghton Mifflin, 1976.

Tolkien, Priscilla and John. *The Tolkien Family Album.* Houghton Mifflin Co., 1992

Wilson, A.N. *C.S. Lewis: A Biography.* New York: W.W. Norton & Company, 1990, 334 p.

1857   Tolkien's father, Arthur Reuel Tolkien, is born.

1870   Tolkien's mother, Mabel Suffield, is born.

1891   Mabel Suffield and Arthur Reuel Tolkien are married in Bloemfontein, South Africa, at the Cape Town Cathedral on April 16.

1892   John Ronald Reuel Tolkien is born in Bloemfontein on January 3.

1894   Tolkien's brother Hilary Arthur Reuel is born on February 17.

1895   Mabel Tolkien and the children return to Birmingham, England; Arthur Tolkien remains in South Africa.

1896   Tolkien's father dies.

1896   Mabel and the children move from Birmingham to Sarehole.

1889   Edith Bratt, Tolkien's future wife, is born in Gloucester on January; Tolkien fails the entrance exam for the King Edward VI School.

1900   Mabel converts to Roman Catholicism.

1900   Tolkien passes the entrance exam for King Edward's; Mabel moves from Sarehole to Mosley in order to be nearer to Birmingham and King Edward's.

1901   Mabel moves the family to a small house near King's Heath Station.

1902   Mabel moves from King's Heath to Edgbaston close to the Birmingham Oratory and enrolls Ronald and Hilary in the Roman Catholic Grammar School of St. Philip.

1903   Tolkien returns to King Edward's on a Foundation Scholarship.

1904   Mabel Tolkien, age 34, dies; Father Francis Xavier Morgan becomes the boys' guardian.

1905   Tolkien and Hilary go to live with their aunt, Beatrice Suffield.

1908 Ronald and Hilary go to live in Mrs. Faulkner's house; Ronald meets Edith Bratt.

1909 Father Francis discovers the romance between Tolkien and Edith; Tolkien fails the scholarship examination for Oxford.

1910 Tolkien and Hilary leave Mrs. Faulkner's for other lodgings; Father Francis forbids all contact with Edith; Edith moves from Birmingham to Cheltenham; In December, Tolkien is awarded an Exhibition Scholarship to Exeter College, Oxford.

1911 T.C.B.S. formed; Tolkien spends his summer holiday in Switzerland; begins at Oxford in autumn; performs in *The Rivals* at King Edward's at Christmas.

1913 Resumes contact with Edith and proposes marriage; passes Oxford Honor Moderation exam with a Second Class; switches to the School of English Language and Literature at Oxford; visits France during summer vacation.

1914 Edith becomes a Roman Catholic, and she and Tolkien are betrothed.

1915 Tolkien is awarded First Class Honors degree in English Language and Literature; He is commissioned as a second lieutenant in the Lancashire Fusiliers.

1916 Tolkien and Edith are married on March 22; Tolkien is sent to France, fights in trenches, contracts "trench fever," and is sent back to England in November.

1917 Begins *The Silmarillion*; son, John, is born.

1918 Discharged from the army; returns to Oxford, works as a lexicographer on the staff of Oxford English Dictionary.

1919 Becomes a freelance tutor at Oxford.

1920 Appointed Reader in English Language at Leeds University; Son, Michael, is born.

1922 With E.V. Gordon begins work on their edition of *Sir Gawain and the Green Knight*.

1924	Appointed Professor of English Language at Leeds; son, Christopher, is born.
1925	*Gawain* is published; elected Rawlinson and Bosworth Professor of Anglo-Saxon at Oxford.
1926	Tolkien forms *The Coalbiters;* meets C.S. Lewis.
1929	Daughter, Priscilla, is born.
c.1930–33	Begins writing The Hobbit.
1936	Delivers the lecture *Beowulf: The Monsters and the Critics.* Finishes *The Hobbit* and Allen & Unwin accepts it for publication.
1937	*The Hobbit* is published. Tolkien begins *The Lord of the Rings.*
1938–39	Writes "Leaf by Niggle;" delivers the lecture "On Fairy-Stories."
1945	Elected Merton Professor of English Language and Literature at Oxford.
1947	"Leaf by Niggle" is published in *The Dublin Review.*
1949	*The Lord of the Rings* is completed. *Farmer Giles of Ham* is published.
1954	*The Fellowship of the Ring* and *The Two Towers*, Volumes I and II of *The Lord of the Rings*, are published.
1955	*The Return of the King*, the last volume of *The Lord of the Rings*, is published.
1957	Offered honorary degrees from Marquette, Harvard, and several other universities in the United States. Edith's ill-health prevents him from accepting.
1959	Retirement from Oxford.
1962	*The Adventures of Tom Bombadil* is published.
1963	C.S. Lewis dies, November 22.
1964	"Leaf by Niggle" and "On Fairy Stories" are published in one volume as *Tree and Leaf.*

1965   Ace Books publishes pirate edition of paperback edition of *The Lord of the Rings* in the United States. Authorized edition follows.

1967   *Smith of Wootton Major* and *The Road Goes Ever On* are published.

1968   Tolkien and Edith move to Poole near Bournemouth.

1971   Edith Tolkien dies at eighty-two on November 29.

1972   Tolkien returns to Oxford as a resident honorary Fellow; Queen Elizabeth II confers upon him the honor of C.B.E., Commander of the British Empire.

1973   Tolkien dies at eighty-one on September 2.

1977   *Silmarillion* published, edited by his son Christopher.

The Fellowship of the Ring (1954)

The Two Towers (1954)

"On Fairy-Stories" in *Tree and Leaf* (1964)

The Adventures of Tom Bombadil (1962).

The Return of the King (1965)

The Hobbit (1966)

Smith of Wootton Major (1967).

The Father Christmas Letters (1976)

The Silmarillion (1977).

Poems and Stories (1980).

Becker, Alida. *The Tolkien Scrapbook.* New York: Grosset & Dunlap, 1978, 192 p.

Birzer, Bradley J. *J.R.R. Tolkien's Sanctifying Myth: Understanding Middle-earth.* ISI Books, 2002, 219 p.

Carpenter, Humphrey. *The Inklings.* Boston: Houghton Mifflin, 1979, 287 p.

———. *Tolkien: A Biography.* Boston: Houghton Mifflin, 1977, 287 p.

———, ed. *The Letters of J.R.R. Tolkien.* With the assistance of Christopher Tolkien. Boston: Houghton Mifflin, 1981, 463 p.

Crabbe, Katharyn. *J.R.R. Tolkien.* New York: The Continuum Publishing Company, Frederick Ungar Publishing Co., Inc., 1988, 233 p.

Garth, John. *Tolkien and the Great War: The Threshold of Middle-earth.* Boston: Houghton Mifflin, 2003, 400 pages.

Grotta-Kurska, Daniel. *J.R.R. Tolkien: Architect of Middle Earth: A Biography.* Edited by Frank Wilson. Philadelphia: Running Press, 1976, 165 p.

Hammond, Wayne G. and Christina Scull. *J R.R. Tolkien: Artist & Illustrator.* Boston: Houghton Mifflin Company, 1995, 208 p.

Helms, Randel. *Tolkien's World.* Boston: Houghton Mifflin, 1974, 167 p.

Lewis, C.S. *Surprised by Joy: The Shape of My Early Life.* New York: Harcourt, Brace & World, Inc., 1955, 238 p.

Moseley, Charles. *J.R.R. Tolkien.* Plymouth, U.K.: Northcote House Publishers, 1997, 95 p.

Rogers, Deborah Webster, and Ivor A. Rogers. *J. R. R. Tolkien.* Boston: Twayne Publishers, 1980, 164 p.

Shippey, T.A. *J.R.R. Tolkien: Author of the Century.* Boston: Houghton Mifflin Company, 2001, 347 p.

Tolkien, Priscilla. "J.R.R. Tolkien and Edith Tolkien's Stay in Staffordshire 1916, 1917 and 1918". In: *Angerthas in English* 3/Angerthas 44. Journal of Arthedain—The Tolkien Society of Norway. Bergen, 1997

Tolkien, Priscilla and John. *The Tolkien Family Album.* Houghton Mifflin Co., 1992

White, Michael. *The Life and Work of J.R.R. Tolkien.* Indianapolis: Alpha Books, 2002, 317 p.

Wilson, A.N. *C.S. Lewis: A Biography.* New York: W.W. Norton & Company, 1990, 334 p.

WEBSITES

www.jrrtolkien.org.uk/homepage.htm

www.tolkienonline.com

www.tolkiensociety.org

http://toosvanholstein.nl/greatwar/tolkien/tolkiene.html

onering.virbius.com/index.php

www.christianitytoday.com/history/

www.nytimes.com/specials/advertising/movies/tolkien

www.simontolkien.com/final%20review/profile.html

NEIL HEIMS is a freelance writer, editor and reasearcher. He has a Ph.D. in English from the City University of New York. He has written on a number of authors including Albert Camus, Arthur Miller, and John Milton.

COLIN DURIEZ is the author of *Tolkien and the Lord of the Rings* and *Tolkien and C.S. Lewis.* He is a featured commentator on *The Lord of the Rings: The Two Towers* DVD Extended Edition.